Dick Turpin

A Pantomime in Two Acts

Paul Reakes

Samuel French — London
New York - Toronto - Hollywood

CAST LIST

Dame Dollop, of Dollop's Farm — *ANTHONY*
Katie Cuddlesome, a milkmaid — *JOANNA*
Billy Bumpkin, a farmhand — *CLIFF*
Daisy, the cow
ALH **Nick**, constable
GRAHAM B **Nab**, constable
Parson Goodfellow
? **Lord Lotaloot**
SAM **Caroline**, Lord Lotaloot's daughter — *DICK*
Dick Turpin, the highwayman
The Judge
GRAHAM ROWSON **Mr X**
Smash, Mr X's accomplice
BM **Grab**, Mr X's accomplice
Chorus of farmhands, milkmaids, villagers, children,
farm animals, party guests and servants

SYNOPSIS OF SCENES

ACT I

ACT II

Other pantomimes by Paul Reakes, published by Samuel French Ltd:
Babes In The Wood
Little Jack Horner
Little Miss Muffet
Old Mother Hubbard
Santa in Space
Sinbad the Sailor

MUSICAL PLOT

ACT I

1	**Song and Dance**	Katie, Chorus, Children and Dancers
2	**Comedy Song** *(optional)*	Dame Dollop
3	**Comedy Duet**	Billy and Katie
4	**Duet and Dance**	Caroline and Dick
	Reprise of No.4 Dance	Katie and Billy
5	**Song and Dance**	Chorus, Children and Dancers
6	**Song**	Chorus
7	**Song and Dance**	Katie, Daisy, Chorus, Children and Dancers
8	**Song and Dance**	Dame, Dick, Billy, Katie, Chorus and Dancers

ACT II

9	**Song and Dance**	Dick, Caroline, Chorus and Dancers
10	**Comedy Song** *(optional)*	Dame, Nick, Nab and Chorus
11	**Song and Dance**	Dick, Caroline, Lotaloot and Dancers
12	**Dance**	Dancers or Children, and Chorus
13	**Duet**	Dick and Caroline
14	**Comedy Trio**	Billy, Dame and Katie
15	**Song and Dance**	All
16	**Sing-a-Long**	Dame, Billy, Daisy and the audience
17	**Final Song**	All

CHARACTERS AND COSTUMES

Pantomime eighteenth century England is the setting for the story.

Dame Dollop is the comical old girl who owns and runs the farm. Her moods change in seconds, and she never misses an opportunity of involving the audience. Her make-up and costumes should be outrageous and funny. Apart from her everyday farm clothes, she gets to wear a ludicrous version of a barrister's outfit with wig and gown, and an outrageous eighteenth century ball gown with a colossal white wig, etc. Finale costume.

Katie Cuddlesome is just as her name implies. A buxom, cuddly darling with rosy cheeks and a pert manner. She hero worships Dick Turpin, and imagines herself in love with the romantic highwayman she has never met. She can be a little spitfire, especially when warding off the amorous advances of Billy Bumpkin. A comedienne's part with singing and dancing ability. Exaggerated rustic accent. Picturesque milkmaid costumes for Act I, and a frilly party outfit for Act II. Finale costume.

Billy Bumpkin is a gormless, but loveable young yokel. He is browbeaten by the Dame and always being shunned by Katie, the love of his life. He provides plenty of comic antics and audience participation. A good singing voice and dancing ability an advantage. Exaggerated rustic accent. In Act I he wears rustic smocks and hats, side button gaiters and heavy boots. In Act II he is seen in a comical, ill fitting "Sunday best" outfit. Finale costume.

Daisy, the cow, is a frisky four-legged friend. She soon becomes a favourite with the audience, especially the youngsters. A good cow skin with moveable mouth, eyelashes and tail. Also, there must be an opening near the "udders" through which to drop the milk bottle, etc. Perhaps a natty straw hat which can be decorated with flowers for the Finale.

Nick and Nab are the comic Constables. Nick is conscientious and duty minded, while Nab is just a loveable buffoon. They provide plenty of comic capers and audience participation. They can be played as a male and female duo if so desired, with the necessary alterations to the script. Their blue uniforms are a comical combination of eighteenth century "Bow Street Runner" and modern police force. Three quarter length, multi-capped tunics and tricorn hats, with chequered edging. Wide belts to hold outsized handcuffs and truncheons.

Parson Goodfellow is really the villainous **Mr X** in disguise! (Both parts being played by the same actor.) This is not revealed until Act II, so please don't let the programme give the game away! Use the actor's real name for the Parson and a pseudonym for Mr X. A virtuoso character actor is needed to portray these two very different roles. Parson Goodfellow is elderly, stooping and frail. He is soft spoken and refined of manner—everyone's idea of the genial, slightly vague old clergyman. Mr X is the complete opposite! Tall and powerful, his movements decisive and threatening, his voice deep and menacing. He never misses an opportunity of goading the audience into a frenzy of boos and hisses!
The costumes: The following is only a suggestion on how to make the change easy. Individual costume designers will have their own ideas. The Parson's eighteenth century all black clerical attire can form a base for both characters. It consists of breeches and stockings, three quarter coat and waistcoat, buckled shoes, white shirt, white neck stock with bands and a round hat. Attached to the inside of the hat is a neck length fringe of white hair. For Mr X's costume, remove the coat, waistcoat, shoes and hat/wig only. These are replaced by riding boots, a long multi-capped riding coat that fastens up the front to the neck (velcro!), a black mask and black tricorn hat. The mask should cover the entire head with openings for eyes and mouth. It is similar to, and could be fashioned from, a modern ski mask. It is advisable to have the two costumes in use early to ensure that the changes are slick.

Lord Lotaloot is a caricature of eighteenth century landed gentry. He is portly, florid and suffers from gout. His pomposity and blustering makes him a rather ridiculous figure. The use of a quizzing glass, and the occasional pinch of snuff would be quite in character. All his clothes are very fine, with powdered wig, embroidered waistcoats, and silk breeches, etc. In Act II he gets to wear a long nightgown and tasselled nightcap.

Caroline is a genteel and beautiful young woman. She has a charming manner and a very nice cleavage! She is forthright and sensible and has a good sense of humour, especially when dealing with her irascible old father. Good singing voice and dancing ability are needed. All her costumes are exquisite eighteenth century, from her daytime clothes in Act I, to her sumptuous ball gown in Act II. Finale costume.

Dick Turpin (Principal boy) is a romanticized version of the legendary highwayman. He is handsome and dashing, with a bold swagger and a magnificent pair of legs! His main concern, apart from falling hopelessly in love with Caroline, is to find the villain who has blackened his good name. To do this, he disguises himself as a farmboy. A strong personality and good singing voice with dancing ability is needed. His highwayman costume consists of: black fishnet tights, thigh boots, shortened brocade waistcoat, white full-sleeved blouse with fancy jabot, black cloak and black tricorn hat. A black half mask, and hair tied back in a black bow complete the picture. For the farmboy disguise, the cloak, hat, boots, waistcoat, jabot and mask are removed and replaced by a rustic jerkin and hat, and buckled shoes. The blouse is worn open at the neck. Finale costume.

The Judge is a caricature of the crusty old justice. He is doddery, deaf and irritated by everyone around him, with the exception of pretty Caroline! His red judicial robe and long curly wig can be liberally sprinkled with dust and cobwebs! An ear trumpet would be a nice touch. He only appears in Act I, Scene 3.

Smash And Grab are Mr X's accomplices in crime. A couple of unsavoury ruffians with unshaven chins, scars and missing teeth. Ideally, Smash should be short, scrawny and cunning, while Grab is huge, hulking and dimwitted. Their outfits are coarse and ragged, a mixture of highwayman and pirate.

The Chorus, Dancers and Children appear as farmhands, milkmaids, farm animals, villagers, village children, party guests and servants. All participate in the action and musical numbers.

PRODUCTION NOTES

Staging

The pantomime offers opportunities for elaborate staging, but can be produced quite simply if facilities and funds are limited. There are five full sets: Dame Dollop's Farmyard, The Courtroom, Kitchen of Dollop's Farm, Ballroom of Lotaloot Hall, and Garden of Lotaloot Hall (this can be used for the Finale). There is one half set: Lord Lotaloot's Bedroom. These scenes are interlinked with tabs or frontcloth scenes. If there is only space to hang one frontcloth, please use it for the "Underground Cell" scenes. The "Outside the Jail" and "Country Lane" scenes can be played to tabs.

The Secret Passages

There are three of them I'm afraid, but the ingenuity of stage managers is amazing! They are all in Act II, and the first we encounter is in the Ballroom scene. It is concealed behind what looks like a large, ornately carved marble fireplace with mantel, surround, and grate, etc. (All made from wood and cleverly painted!) This unit is hinged so that it opens into the room like a door. Behind it is an opening in the back wall flat. It would be nice to have an eerie creaking effect as the fireplace opens and shuts! The second passage is in the garden scene. It is concealed behind the back wall of a stone alcove. A painted flat that slides easily when operated by the backstage crew should suffice. In Lord Lotaloot's bedroom scene there are two bookcases concealing the third passage. These are simply two ordinary door flats set in the back wall and painted (cleverly!) to resemble well filled book shelves. The "doors" open into the room and should remain open when necessary. All the openings should be backed by black flats or curtains. It is advisable to have all these "secret passage" pieces of scenery well in use before the actual performance.

Dick Turpin's Entrance in the Courtroom

This should be as startling and dramatic as you can make it. If facilities allow, he could drop from above on a rope, or appear through a trap door in the stage! A simple way would be to have Dick make his entrance from the back of the auditorium, firing off his pistol as he does so. NOTE: Special care must be paid to the firing of blanks and a note in the programme stating that guns are fired during a performance is strongly advisable.

The Table Manners Lesson
A slapstick routine for the Dame, Nick and Nab, and Billy. The choice of the comic business is left to the individual director, but it must be well thought out and well rehearsed. If desired, the whole routine can be cut. After Nab's line "An' everyone knows you use a knife" he and Nick exit L, and Dick enters R, going straight into "'Ello, Dame Dollop! Oi've brought you a visitor."

The Fencing Duel
This must be exciting, spectacular and above all, believable. Please don't let it be just a few timid strokes with the swords and all over! It may be worth calling on the services of a professional fencing instructor to help your duellists make it look really convincing.

P. R.

ACT I

Dame Dollop's Farmyard

UR *is a thatched farmhouse with a practical front door.* UL, *a wooden barn with practical doors. Across the back, a low rustic fence with an opening in the centre. Tree and outhouse side wings. The backcloth and ground row show fields, hay ricks, etc. Bales of straw and farming implements are dotted about*

When the CURTAIN *rises, the farmhands, children and the dancers are discovered. They go straight into the opening song and dance. As part of this number, Katie Cuddlesome dances on with a feed pail. She is followed by two of the senior dancers as a hen and a cockerel. They perform a short dance, then the cock crows loudly. On this command, a troupe of junior dancers file on as little chicks. They dance, and are then led out by the cockerel. One "stage-struck" little chick remains and has to be chased out by the hen. Katie and the others end the number with a tableau*

Song 1

Dame (*yelling from inside the house*) Bumpkin! Billy Bumpkin! Where are ya?!

Katie (*to the others*) Look out! 'Ere's Dame Dollop! You lot better watch out. She be in a right old temper this mornin'!

Woman Why be that then, Katie?

Katie Billy Bumpkin be gone missin' again! 'Tis the third time this week!

Man Cor! Oi'd 'ate to be in 'is shoes when Old Dollop gets 'old of 'im!

Dame (*from the house*) Bumpkin!

Katie 'Ere she comes! Look busy!

They scatter and pretend to be busy about the yard

Dame Dollop storms out of the house

Dame (*moving* C; *fuming*) Billy Bumpkin! Where is that lazy, loafin'
layabout?! Oh, just wait till I get 'old of 'im! I'll slaughter 'im! I'll do
'im a mischief! I'll cut off 'is privileges! I'll… I'll (*the ultimate cruelty*)
give 'im a one way ticket to (*local place*)!

Katie Baint 'e turned up yet, missus?

Dame Turned up! Turned up! I'll turn 'im up when I get me 'ands on 'im!
I pay 'im to *work* on this farm! Ten pence a week and as much cow cake
as 'e can eat! I don't pay 'im to go AWOL all the time! (*To the audience*)
I can't understand it! I mean… (*To the others*) I'm not a 'ard boss to
work for, am I?

The others look away, whistle, etc

All right! All right! Don't take a flippin' vote on it! (*To the audience*)
No, I'm a smashin' boss. I'm always there to listen to folks' problems.

One of the men doubles over with surprised laughter

Always there to… (*She becomes aware of the man. To him*) And what
do you find so funny, Mr Blobby? Don't you think I'm a good boss?

Man Ar, Dame Dollop! Oi can't imagine another boss like you…

Dame (*to the audience; very pleased*) See!

Man (*aside to the audience*) Unless it were—(*topical nasty*)!

Dame (*to the others*) Well, don't just stand there like rejects from (*local
gag*). Go and find Billy Bumpkin! And don't come back without the
lazy so-and-so! Go on!

Katie and the others run out in all directions

(*To the audience*) Well, what do you think of my little farm? Nice, isn't
it. It's much better than all the others around 'ere! They're all—arable!
Oh, please yerselves! Do any of you know anythin' about farmin'? Oh,
I know! You've all watched *Emmerdale* and listened to *The Archers*!
Well, it's not a bit like that. I've got to do things 'ere that would make
Joe Sugden 'ang up 'is wellies for good! Every day I'm up at crack of
dawn, lookin' after the livestock. I've got to give all the hens a hug, all
the sheep a cuddle, and all the cows a pat! (*She inspects the bottom of
her shoe*) As if they didn't have enough of them already! Farmin' is 'ard
work, but I love it! I live and breathe it! (*She takes a deep breath, then*

sniffs) Pooh! That reminds me, I must get a new can of *Glade* for that pigsty!

Song 2 *(optional)*

After the song, Dame Dollop moves DR *to tidy some implements*

Katie enters at the back with Parson Goodfellow, a benign old clergyman

Katie *(calling to Dame Dollop)* Missus! Look who be 'ere!
Dame *(straightening up without looking around)* So! You've found that idle good for nothin', 'ave ya! Bring 'im 'ere!

As she rants on, Katie and the Parson move down C

Now, listen to me you dozy dunderhead! You're a waste of space! You're about as much use as a chocolate coffee pot.

Katie, unable to contain her laughter any longer, rushes out L

And another thing! If brains were dynamite you wouldn't 'ave enough to blow yer 'at off! In short, you're a dopey, soppy, silly great useless idle twit! *What* are ya?! (*She turns and comes face to face with the Parson. She reacts and staggers back*) Holy smoke!
Parson *(still smiling benignly)* Good morning, Dame Dollop. So pleased to make your acquaintance. My name is Goodfellow. I am your new parson.
Dame *(aside to the audience)* New?! 'E looks old enough to be Fred Flintstone's grandad! (*To him, gushing*) Oh, charmed ever so, your ecclesiasticalness! But what 'appened to the other one? Parson Pewfiller.
Parson *(shaking his head)* Ah, very sad. I am afraid the poor man had to retire through ill health. The bells were his undoing, I'm sorry to say. (*He sighs*)
Dame Bell's whisky?
Parson Church bells. He had many, many problems with them. Do you know, he had to have his "Big Tom" rehung several times?
Dame Get away! Come to think of it, he always seemed a bit highly strung!
Parson Sadly it prayed upon his health and forced him to take early retirement at *(local holiday resort)*.

Dame Oh, I went there once, but it was shut! (*She guffaws loudly at her "joke" and gives him a playful push, almost knocking him over*) Whoops! Sorry! Mustn't *knock* the church! (*She laughs again*)

Parson Ah, Dame Dollop, a good sense of humour is indeed a great blessing.

Dame You're right! (*She indicates the audience*) Try tellin' *them* that! So! You're the new parson, are ya?

Parson Yes, but I have been consecrated here for several months now.

Dame Oo! I'm sorry to 'ear that. I swear by All-Bran meself!

A noise is heard off L. *It is Nick and Nab making the sound of a police car siren. Startled, the Dame and Parson clear to* DR

To suitable police theme music, Nick and Nab run on from L. *They are miming sitting together in a car with Nick doing the "driving". Nab has a blue flashing light fixed to the top of his hat. They do a couple of circuits of the stage, loudly making the siren noise*

Katie and the farmhands rush on excitedly from the back

Finally, Nick and Nab stop the "car", and the siren's wail dies. They "get out", then stand together doing an exaggerated knee bending routine

Nick ⎫
Nab ⎭ (*together; bending knees*) Mornin' all!

Dame (*to the audience*) Let that be a warnin'! Never buy underpants from (*local shop or mail order catalogue*)! (*She moves to them*) Why, if it isn't our answer to *Sun Hill*. What can I do for you two blue bottles?

Nab We've come to stick it up!

Dame (*aghast*) I beg your pardon!

Nick This! (*He whips a large, rolled-up poster from his tunic*)

He and Nab unroll it. It is a "Wanted" poster with large printing and crude portrait of Dick Turpin

(*Reading*) "Wanted! Dead or alive. Dick Turpin, the notorious highwayman! Reward five hundred pounds!"

They hold it up for all to see. General reaction

Katie (*pushing forward, horrified*) Dick Turpin! Dead or alive! Ooo! (*She bursts into tears, and runs wailing to Dame Dollop for comfort*)
Dame Now, don't take on so, Katie! It 'ad to come sooner or later the way 'e's been carryin' on.

Katie wails even louder and buries her face in Dame Dollop's bosom

'Ere! Steady on! You'll give me wet rot in the whatnot!
Parson (*concerned*) Pray, what ails the poor child?
Dame Oh, she's just bein' a silly billy. Fancy gettin' all upset over a nasty highwayman!
Katie (*pulling away with tearful indignation*) Dick Turpin *baint* nasty! 'E be romantic an' dashin' an' 'andsome an' ... an' (*She turns on Nick and Nab*) Oi don't believe 'e done all them 'orrible things!
Nick Well, we find it hard to believe ourselves.
Nick A few months ago he'd just rob the odd coach, steal a few pounds and nobody got hurt. But now it's robbery with violence! The hospital is full of casualties from his crimes! I'm sorry to say that Dick Turpin, the once lovable rogue, has turned into a real nasty piece of work!

The others agree

Katie (*wailing*) It baint true! Oi don't believe it! Oi *won't* believe! Oi won't! Oi won't!

Wailing loudly, she rushes out L

Parson Oh, goodness me!
Dame Take no notice, your Parsnip. 'Er 'ead's full of romantic rubbish. She's not been the same since (*recent romantic event in popular TV soap*)!
First Woman I can understand why Katie feels so upset.
Second Woman (*getting "all romantic"*) Ooo, so can I! We all had a soft spot for the *old* Dick Turpin!

All the women give a deep sigh

Nick Well, he's a changed man now and we've got to bring him in dead or alive! That's the law and our duty is to carry out the law! (*He salutes*)
Nab And may the force be with you! (*He salutes comically*)

Nick (*to Dame Dollop, holding up the poster*) Where shall I put this?
Dame (*to the audience*) Oo! Shall I tell 'im, folks? No! No! I don't want
to be run in for causin' an obstruction, do I! (*To Nick*) Put it on the barn
door.

*Nick and Nab bend their knees and salute. During the following dialogue,
they move up and fix the poster to the barn door*

(*Sidling up to Parson*) Now, your Sermonship, what would you say to
a little nibble? Per'aps a cup of tea and a slice of somethin' (*she flutters
her eyelashes*) wholesome!
Parson (*flustered and edging away*) Well, I don't...
Dame (*moving in closer*) I'm sure I could tempt you with one of my roly-
poly puddin's. (*She pushes her chest out*)
Parson S—so kind ... er ... but, I have other calls ... yes ... good
morning!

Parson makes a hasty exit DR

Dame (*to the audience*) Well, 'e's too old for me anyway!

*Having put up the poster, Nick and Nab move down and mime getting
into the "car" and starting it up. Making the siren noise, they run out* L

(*Rounding on the farmhands*) Oy, you lot! I thought I told you to find
that lazy layabout, Billy Bumpkin! Go on, get lookin'! Now! Move!

They run out calling "Billy! Billy Bumpkin, where are you" etc.

Dame Dollop exits into the house

A slight pause

*The barn doors open slowly and the sleepy figure of Billy Bumpkin
emerges. He has straw sticking to his hat and smock. He stretches,
yawns and rubs his eyes. He catches sight of the audience and ambles
down to greet them*

Billy (*to the audience, calling and waving*) Marnin'!

A few replies

Coo! You lot be more asleep than wot oi be! (*He calls louder*) Marnin'!

They shout back

Thas better! Oi bet you don't know who oi be?

Comic by-play with audience

No, an' oi baint (*current heart-throb*) either! 'E baint as good lookin'!
Oi be Billy Bumpkin! Dame Dollop's right 'and man on the farm. Coo!
Oi've jus' bin 'avin' a smashin' kip in the barn! (*He chuckles*) Oi bet ole
Dollop ain't even noticed oi were missin', 'ave she?

"Yes" from the audience

Oh no, she, 'aven't!

Routine with the audience

Wull, oi don't care! (*Slyly*) Oi were 'avin' a dream about Katie
Cuddlesome, the milkmaid! 'Ave you seen 'er yet? Cor! Proper little
smasher, baint she?! (*All sloppy*) Oi be in love wi' 'er, oi be! Oi loves
every thing about 'er from 'er little nose to 'er little toes! (*Slyly*) An' all
they other little bits in between! Cor...! (*He looks off* L) 'Ere she comes
now! (*He moves down* R, *and smartens himself up*)

Katie enters from L. *She does not see Billy, and goes directly to look at
the poster. She gazes adoringly at it and gives a couple of huge sighs*

(*Edging nervously towards her, screwing up his hat*) K—K—Katie!
Katie (*turning with a start*) Oh...! (*Annoyed at seeing who it is*) Oh, 'tis
only *you*, Billy Bumpkin! You made oi jump, you gurt fool you!
Billy (*following her*) W—why were you lookin' at that picture an' makin'
they funny noises?
Katie (*turning sharply*) What funny noises?
Billy You know— (*he does an exaggerated copy of Katie's sighs*) Like
that.

Katie (*rattled*) None o' your business! (*She flounces over to* R)

Billy (*peering at the poster*) Why, dangle me breeches! That be a picture o' Dick Turpin, the highwayman!

Katie gazes out front and sighs deeply as before

(*Rushing down to her*) 'Ere! You'm doin' 'em again! They be *lovesick* noises, they be! Like wot oi makes when oi looks at you!

Katie (*sarcastic*) Oh, oi always thought you 'ad indigestion!

Billy Why be you makin' lovesick noises over Dick Turpin? (*Jokingly*) You baint in love wi' 'e, be ee?

Katie (*firmly*) Yes, oi be!

Billy (*laughing, then double take*) 'Ave you met 'im, then?

Katie (*sadly*) No!

Billy B—but you be in love wi' 'im?

Katie (*rapturously*) Oh, ar!

Billy (*to the audience, dismayed*) An' they call *oi* the village idiot! (*To her*) Ha! Oi know wot you'm up to, Katie Cuddlesome! You'm tryin' to make oi jealous!

Katie (*sharply*) Jealous?!

Billy Ar! You knows oi loves ee! Oi'd do anythin' fer ee, Katie! Jus' say you loves oi back! (*He goes to embrace her*) Give oi a kiss!

Katie (*pushing him away and laughing scornfully*) Love *you*! Ha! You be a nothin', you be Billy Bumpkin! I loves a *real* man! (*Rapturously*) Dick Turpin! 'E's 'andsome! 'E's dashin'! E's romantic! E's...

Billy (*pointing to poster*) Wanted—dead or alive!

Katie (*moving away, on the verge of tears*) Oh, shut up!

Billy (*going to her*) Katie! My little bumble bee! Forget about Dick Turpin... 'E'll only come to a bad end. Oi could make ee ever so 'appy, if only you'd let oi!

Song 3

A comedy duet. Billy tries to woo Katie and proclaim his attributes. She merely ridicules him at every opportunity. After the song, he tries to embrace her. She pushes him away, and he falls over

(*Sitting up*) Oh, Katie! Oi'd ... oi'd *kill* meself fer you!

Katie Don't bother! When Dame Dollop gets 'old o' you, she'll save ee the trouble!

Katie stomps out L

Billy (*getting up and calling after her*) Old Dollop don't worry oi! (*To the audience, playing the tough guy*) Oi baint scared o' she! Oi be a strong, fearless chap. Like that Arnie Schwarzenthingummy. Look at they muscles! (*He flexes his arms*)

Dame Dollop comes out of the house. She sees Billy and creeps up behind him, rolling up her sleeves ready for action

Jus' let old Dollop try an' boss oi about! Oi'll show the old droopy drawers! If she were 'ere now oi'd give 'er a right ear bashin'! Oi'd say to 'er——
Dame Yes? What would you say?
Billy (*gulping in horror*) Oi ... oi'd say...
Dame Yes?
Billy Oi'd say—what a lovely, gorgeous creature you were!
Dame (*roaring*) You!

Billy gives a terrified wail and goes to make a run for it. Dame Dollop grabs the end of his smock. Comic business as he runs on the spot, getting nowhere fast. Eventually he flops to the ground exhausted. Dame Dollop hauls him to his feet

(*Rapidly*) Where 'ave you been? What 'ave you been doin? Why weren't you workin'?!
Billy Oi...
Dame Don't answer me back! Oh, you useless lump! I don't know why I put up with you! 'Ave you milked Daisy the cow this mornin'?
Billy Nope!
Dame Why not?
Billy Cos she don't like it up North.
Dame Up North?
Billy Ar! She don't like 'er—*Uddersfield*! (*He guffaws loudly*)

Dame Dollop is stone faced. He reacts and the laughter dies

Dame Well, she's got to be milked. (*She looks about*) Where is the silly old cow?
Billy (*under his breath and giving her a side glance*) Not far away.

Dame (*catching the look and grabbing him*) Watch it! Watch it! Where is she?
Billy In the field ... readin' the paper.
Dame What paper?
Billy The *moos* of the world! (*He guffaws again*)

Dame Dollop clips him around the ear

Dame (*calling*) Daisy! Daisy!
Billy (*singing*) Give me your answer do!

She takes a swing at him. He ducks and laughs, but she gets him on the rebound

Dame (*to the audience*) Kids, will you 'elp us call for Daisy? Ta! After three! One, two, three...

They call "Daisy" a couple of times

   To suitable music, Daisy the cow trots on from L

   There she is! (*She goes to the cow*) Hullo, Daisy dear!
Daisy (*nestling up to Dame Dollop*) Mooo!
Dame (*hugging her*) Ahh! She loves me! (*To the audience*) She thinks I'm 'er mummy!
Billy (*to the audience*) Ar! We kin see the resemblance!
Dame Now, Daisy dear, give all the nice people a big curtsy.

Daisy turns her back on the audience and curtsies to the backcloth

Billy (*to the audience*) That's wot she thinks o' you lot!
Dame (*taking Daisy's tail and speaking down it*) Hullo! Dame Dollop to base! Are you receivin' me? (*She puts the end of the tail to her ear*)
Daisy Mooo!
Dame (*yelling down the tail*) Round the other way, dear!

Daisy turns to face the front and curtsies

   (*To the audience*) Isn't she a clever girl? Now, Daisy, it's milkin' time, an' you like bein' milked, don't you?

Daisy shakes her head

Oh yes, you do! Now, Mummy'll fetch the bucket, and Uncle Billy'll fetch the stool. (*She goes* R *to get the bucket—plastic*)

Billy goes L *to get the stool. Daisy starts to creep backwards. They see her and bring her back down stage*

Billy 'Ere! Why 'as a milkin' stool only got three legs?
Dame 'Cos—the cow's got the *udder*! (*To the audience*) You were waitin' for that one, weren't you?! (*To Billy*) Let's get on with it! (*She places the bucket on the ground, steps back, and points it out to Daisy*)

Daisy takes a run at it and kicks the bucket away

Billy Goal! (*To the audience*) The (*local football team*) could use 'er!

Dame Dollop retrieves the bucket

Dame Oh, Daisy, you naughty girl! (*To Billy*) Don't just stand there, *do* somethin'!
Billy (*putting down the stool and sitting on it*) Come on, Daisy old girl! (*He slaps his thighs*) Milkin' time! Oi be waitin'!

Daisy goes to him and sits her rear end in his lap. He yells. Daisy jumps up and frisks about. Billy gets up with his legs crossed and hobbles about in agony. Dame Dollop catches Daisy and places the bucket under her. Billy grabs the cow's tail and starts working it like a pump

Dame Anything?
Billy (*looking in the bucket*) Nothin'! 'Ere! It must be—*evaporated* milk! (*He doubles over with laughter*)

Daisy kicks him with her hind leg and knocks him over

Dame Oh! Let me try! (*She pumps Daisy's tail*)

A bottle of milk drops into the bucket! Billy holds it up and he and the Dame cheer. Daisy moos. Dame Dollop pumps again. A box of chocolates drops into the bucket! Billy holds it up

Ooo! Lovely! A box of Milk Tray! (*She pats Daisy*) Well done, Daisy dear!

Billy Be there anythin' else to come down?

Daisy shakes her head and stamps her foot defiantly

Dame All right! All right! Don't get yer teats in a tangle! (*She pats her*) I think you've done very well! (*To the audience*) Didn't she do well, boys and girls?

"Yes!" from the audience

Come on! Give Daisy a clap!

Daisy bows to all parts of the house as they applaud. Dame Dollop picks up the bucket and stool. Billy has the milk bottle and box of chocolates

I'll take charge of that! That's farm property! (*She holds out the bucket*) 'And it over!

He hides the box behind his back and drops the bottle into the bucket

And the choccies!

He reluctantly puts them in the bucket

Billy Oi thought you was tryin' to diet!

Dame Wrong! I'm dying to try it! (*She goes to the house*) Go on! Take Daisy back to 'er field!

Dame Dollop exits into the house

Daisy goes to Billy and nestles up to him

Billy (*hugging her; then sadly*) Wull, 'tis nice to know *one* girl loves oi! Come on, Daisy.

Billy leads Daisy out L

A commotion is heard off stage. In a state of near collapse, Lord Lotaloot staggers on at the back. He is being supported on one side by

*Parson Goodfellow, and a pretty young milkmaid on the other. Caroline
and some of the farmhands follow. The others rush on from the sides*

Lotaloot (*staggerring down* c, *and wailing*) Ooo! I have been robbed!
Robbed! ROBBED! Oo! (*He sags against the milkmaid for comfort*)
Caroline (*unruffled, quite used to his tantrums*) Father, pray compose
yourself.
Lotaloot (*exploding*) Compose myself! Zounds! Daughter, I have been
robbed! Broken into! Vandalized! (*He wails*) Oooo! (*He sags against
the Parson, realizes his mistake and sags against the milkmaid again*)
Parson But *who* has robbed you, my lord?
Lotaloot (*resurfacing again*) Who?! Why, that devil of course! That
blackguard! That monster—Dick Turpin! (*He wails, and seeks comfort
from the milkmaid again*) Oo! Robbed! *Robbed!* ROBBED!

Dame Dollop storms out of the house

Dame Oy! Oy! Oy! What's all this noise in my farmyard?! What's
goin' on?
Lotaloot (*swallowing in self pity*) I have been plundered!
Dame Well, go an' see a doctor about it! Don't come 'ere makin' that row
an' wearin' that candyfloss on yer 'ead! You'll put me hens off layin'!
Parson Dame Dollop, this is Lord Lotaloot and his daughter, the
honourable Miss Caroline.
Lotaloot My coach has just been held up by that villain Dick Turpin! He
robbed me of every penny I possess!
Caroline My father is inclined to exaggerate. 'Tis true the highwayman
relieved him of his purse, but to my knowledge it only contained two
guineas. Is that not so, Father?
Lotaloot (*blustering*) I—I... (*Saving face*) Egad! Highway robbery is
highway robbery! Turpin must be caught and hung! The dashed fellow
is a menace! A fiend in human shape!
Caroline (*taking a purse from her bag and holding it up for all to see*) *My*
purse, however, contains *fifty* guineas. It is money intended for the poor
and needy of the parish. When I informed Dick Turpin of the fact, he
bade me keep it. He also kindly donated the two guineas he had just
taken from my father.
Parson 'Tis hardly the actions of a "fiend in human shape".
Caroline Quite so. I would call it the actions of a gentleman. (*Wistfully*)
A very charming gentleman.

Man Ar! It do sound more like the *old* Dick Turpin!

The others agree

Lotaloot Gadzooks! You would turn this scoundrel into a saint! I have
  been robbed, remember that! I demand justice! The law must be
  invoked! Send for the constables immediately!
Dame (*to the others*) Well, go on, you lot! You 'eard 'is nibs! Run an'
  fetch—(*popular TV/film police duo*)! Go on!

  The farmhands run out in all directions

The milkmaid remains, still supporting and comforting Lotaloot

  (*Going to her*) That includes *you*, Miss Bedpan! 'E's bin "held up"
  enough for one day! 'Op it!

  The girl gives her a look and runs out

Dame Dollop takes over supporting Lotaloot

  Now, your circumference, you must be feelin' proper pooped. While
  we're waitin', why don't you come to my 'umble 'ovel and take the
  weight off yer wallet.

She leads him to the house and opens the door

Lotaloot Come Caroline! Join me within.
Caroline If it please you both, I wish to stay and enjoy the beautiful fresh
  air and sunshine. I shall remain without.
Lotaloot But...
Dame Oh, leave 'er be! If she wants to go without that's 'er 'ard luck! You
  won't find me so finicky!

  *She gives him a nudge and a wink, then pushes him into the house. She
  is about to go in herself when she notices that the Parson is about to
  follow*

  Yes?
Parson (*indicating that he too should enter*) I thought...

Dame Sorry, Rev! You 'ad your chance!

The Dame exits, slamming the door in his face

Rather taken aback, Parson exits DR

Caroline (*to the audience, sighing*) Oh, lackaday! What a dilemma I find myself in to be sure. I confess I have fallen hopelessly in love with a total stranger! Under ordinary circumstances this would be perplexing enough; but he is a notorious highwayman! A wanted criminal! Oh, is this really happening to me, or is it just some wild dream?

Song 4

As Caroline starts to sing, the Lighting becomes "magical and dream-like". A little carefully controlled ground mist would help

The romantic, masked figure of Dick Turpin enters

He joins Caroline in the song, then they waltz together. Perhaps the chorus could take up the song off stage as they dance. They end the duet with a kiss

Dick retreats up stage to vanish from sight

All this must appear to have happened to Caroline in a dream. The Lighting returns to normal

Dazed and enchanted, Caroline exits into the house

Dick Turpin emerges from behind the barn and moves stealthily down. He looks towards the house and proclaims sadly

Dick Aye, then 'tis true! There is such a thing as love at first sight! (*He sighs, then snapping out of the mood, addresses the audience in a bold, swaggering manner*) Goodmorrow, friends! Bold Dick Turpin at your service! (*A flamboyant bow*) Of late, some cowardly rogue has been committing hideous crimes and blaming them on me! But fear not! I have a plan that will right the foul wrongs done to me. In the guise of a common labourer I propose to seek employment at this very farm. Under this deception I hope to discover the villain's identity and thus clear my good name! Adieu, my friends! When next we meet I shall no longer be Dick Turpin, Prince of Highwaymen, but plain Dick Appleseed, a common rustic!

Dick bows and exits into the barn

Nick and Nab are heard making the siren noises off L. They "drive" on as before, followed by the farmhands

Dame Dollop, Lotaloot and Caroline come out of the house

Comic business with Nick and Nab "pulling up", the siren dying and knee bending routine. Lotaloot peers at them through his quizzing glass

Lotaloot (*to Dame Dollop, with disgust*) Are *these* the officers of the law?!
Dame What did you expect—Batman and Robin?
Lotaloot I am Lord Lotaloot and I have just been robbed by Dick Turpin!
Nick ⎫
            (*together; bending knees*) Yes, m'lud!
Nab ⎭
Lotaloot Well, don't just bob up and down, like that! Find the rogue! Do your duty! Seek him out!

Nick and Nab spring into action. Nab goes down on all fours and starts sniffing around everyone like a bloodhound. Nick whips out an enormous magnifying glass and examines Dame Dollop and Lotaloot. Comic business

Finally, Nick and Nab "drive" out making the siren noise, followed by the farmhands

During the following dialogue, Dick sneaks unseen from the barn. He has discarded the cloak, mask, etc. and now wears a short rustic jerkin and hat

Come Caroline, let us return to the Hall! Zounds! All this vexation! I fear an attack of the gout at any moment!
Dame Don't worry, your battleship! It's at the vet's.

Lotaloot What is?

Dame The goat!

Lotaloot (*hotly*) I said *gout*, woman! Gout! Gout! (*Exasperated, he stamps his foot, then yells with agony*) Ahh! There! I told you so! (*He hobbles about in pain*) Ooo! Help me, Caroline!

Dame (*rushing to assist*) Allow me! (*In her eagerness she steps on his foot*)

He wails and hops about on one leg. Dame Dollop finds this amusing and starts doing a Highland fling and singing "The Campbells are Comin'". Enraged, Lotaloot hobbles to a bale of straw and sits, nursing his foot. Dick comes forward and Dame Dollop dances into him

Dick (*cheerfully, with a broad rustic accent*) Marnin'!

Dame Crikey! Where did you spring from?

Dick (*touching his forelock*) Dick Appleseed be my name! Farm labourin' be my game! 'Ave you got a vacant position?

Dame (*shocked*) 'Ere! Don't be personal...! Oh, I get it! You're lookin' for a job on the farm.

Dick Ar!

Dame What can you do?

Dick (*proudly*) Oi can do it all! (*Hands on hips*) Oi be your man!

Dame (*to the audience*) Funny lookin' *man*! Must be from (*local place*)! (*She circles Dick, giving him the "once over"*)

Caroline (*to the audience*) This fellow seems strangely familiar. His actions ... his voice. He reminds me of ... no, I am just being foolish...

Lotaloot Caroline! Help me up, and let us be gone from here!

Caroline helps Lotaloot up and assists him up stage

Dick (*moving to them*) Can oi be of any assistance?

Caroline Er... No, thank you. I can manage, Mr...

Dick (*removing his hat*) Appleseed. 'Umble Dick Appleseed at your service. (*He takes her hand and gives it a long kiss*)

Lotaloot and Dame Dollop react

Lotaloot (*at last, with a disapproving cough*) Ah hem! Caroline, when you've quite finished letting this fellow wash your hand, I'd like to return home!

*Caroline gently retrieves her hand and moves to the centre opening with
Lotaloot. She stops and looks back at Dick. He gives her a low bow*

   Lotaloot tugs at Caroline and they exit at the back

Dame (*to the still bowing Dick*) You can take the strain off yer braces now,
   she's gone!

Dick straightens up

   So, you want a job on my farm, eh?
Dick Ar, please, missus.
Dame Well, let's go into the house and take down yer particulars.

They move to the house. She opens the door, then stops to look at him

   Are you sure you've done farm work before?
Dick Oh, ar! Reapin', sowin', 'edgin', ditchin', milkin', ploughin'! Oi
   can do the lot!
Dame (*archly*) In them stockings?
Dick Oh, ar!
Dame What 'appens if you get a ladder?
Dick Oi can use it to climb the 'ayricks!

   *He exits into the house. Dame Dollop does a double take, gives the
   audience a look, and follows him in*

Billy (*off* L) Katie...! Come back 'ere...!

   Katie flounces on from L, *hotly pursued by Billy*

   (*Grabbing her arm*) Katie Cuddlesome, you bide still an' listen to oi!
Katie (*pulling free*) Get yer paws off oi, you gurt booby!
Billy (*falling on his knees before her*) Katie, oi love 'ee!
Katie Wull, oi don't love *you*! Oi be in love wi' (*rapturously*) Dick
   Turpin!

   Katie sighs deeply as before, then drifts off DR

Billy (*pursuing her on his knees*) Katie...! Come back...! Katie...!

She has gone

Oh, dung flies! (*He gets to his feet*) Dick Turpin! Pah! (*To the audience, dejected*) Oi give up, folks! 'Tis a waste o' time! Chasin' after 'er 'ave made oi proper tired again! (*He gives a big yawn*) Oi be goin' to 'ave another kip in the barn! (*He looks towards the house, then sneaks up to the barn and opens the door. He sees something inside and reacts*) 'Ere! Wot be that? (*He reaches in and pulls out Dick's cloak, hat and mask*) A cloak...! A mask...! Wot be they doin' in... (*He catches sight of the poster and compares the items to it*) Dangle oi in a dung 'eap! 'Tis just like the ones Dick Turpin wears! Oi wonder how... (*He is suddenly struck with an idea and gives a wide grin*) Ar! If Katie wants Dick Turpin, she can 'ave 'im!

Billy quickly goes into the barn and shuts the door

Reprise of No 4. Dance

The music starts, and Katie dances on from DR. *She dances alone for a while, then Billy emerges from the barn. He is now wearing the cloak, hat and mask. He joins Katie in the dance and it turns into a clumsy, comic version. Amazingly, Katie is convinced she is in the arms of the man of her dreams! It ends with Billy holding Katie in a Valentino type embrace*

After the applause, Nick and Nab enter from L. *They pull up short at seeing the couple*

Katie (*gazing up at Billy; breathlessly*) Are you...?
Billy (*doing his best to disguise his voice and sound macho, but it comes out toneless and stilted*) Aye! 'Tis I! Dick Terrapin ... er... Turpin! I have risked life and limb to come here and declare my love for you!
Katie (*in paradise*) Dick Turpin! Oh, my 'ero...! (*She faints in his arms*)

Nick and Nab shake with fear. Nab makes a run for it, but Nick pulls him back. Summoning their courage, they creep towards Billy who is having great trouble holding Katie up

Nick (*in a quiet, timid voice*) D—D—Dick Turpin. You are under ... arrest! (*He puts a tentative hand on Billy's shoulder*)

Billy yells with fright. So do Nick and Nab. Billy lets Katie fall to the ground, where she wakes, sits up and wails. Panicking, Billy makes a run for it. "Chase" music. Nick and Nab pursue Billy around the stage, blowing their police whistles

The farmhands run on from all directions. At the same time, the Parson enters DR, *and Dame Dollop and Dick rush from the house*

Bedlam! Eventually, Nick and Nab seize Billy and hold him firmly. The music and noise stop

(*Gasping*) We've … caught … him!
Nab (*gasping*) We've … caught … Dick Turpin!

General reaction. Billy is too exhausted and confused to say anything. Katie rushes to Dame Dollop. Dick is puzzled, but secretly amused

Nick (*finding his voice of authority*) Dick Turpin, I arrest you in the name of the law!
Dame At last we can find out who Dick Turpin *really* is! Take off 'is mask!

Nick and Nab pull away the hat and mask to reveal a terrified Billy. General sensation

All Billy Bumpkin!

Music and uproar. Katie faints into the arms of Dick. Dame Dollop faints into the arms of the Parson and Billy into the arms of Nick and Nab. The music reaches a dramatic crescendo

Black-out

SCENE 2

Outside the Jail

Tabs, or a frontcloth showing a street and part of the jail house with its narrow, barred windows and heavy, studded door

Nick and Nab enter from the jail side

Nick (*very pleased with himself*) Well, that's Dick Turpin safely behind
  bars! I reckon we'll get promotion for this bit of police work! (*He puffs
  out his chest*) I could be CID!
Nab C—I—D? SID! I thought your name was Nickelarse!

Nick hits him

  Oy! Stop doin' that! You're always hittin' me about! It's not fair, (*to the
  audience*) is it? (*By-play with audience, then to Nick*) You know what'll
  'appen if you keep knockin' me about like that?
Nick No, what?
Nab I'll turn into a "bent" copper! (*He sniggers*)

Nick hits him, knocking him flat on the ground

Nick Now you're a "sleeping policeman"!
Nab (*getting to his feet*) Anyway, he says he's not Dick Turpin. Just Billy
  Bumpkin, a fully paid-up member of the village idiot society. He
  reckons it was a mistake and he's innocent.
Nick Ha! They all say that! Well, he goes on trial tomorrow! That'll prove
  whether he's innocent or not.
Nab (*shivering*) Oo! It must be 'orrible bein' locked up in that nasty little
  cell! D'you know, even the rats have moved out! No proper ... er, you
  know... (*He mimes pulling a chain*) It's enough to make a man go potty!
  An' no entertainment either! No *Neighbours* or *Home and Away*!
Nick In that case, I think I'll move in *with* him!

*Dame Dollop enters from the street side. She wears another outrageous
costume and is carrying a large, bulging shopping bag*

Dame (*to the audience*) Hullo, folks! (*Confidentially*) There's those two
  nitwits! I'll 'ave to butter 'em up if I want to get in and see Billy. (*To
  them, gushing and saucy*) Hullo, you two beautiful boys in blue!
Nick ⎫
       ⎬ (*together; bending knees*) Mornin'!
Nab ⎭
Dame Still got the old trouble I see. You should try WD40.
Nick What can I do for you, madam?

Dame (*seductive and fluttering her eyelashes*) Well, what have you got to offer? (*She gives him a playful nudge*) D'you know, you remind me of that dishy young policeman in "Heartburn".

Nick (*flattered*) Oh, do you think so, I ... surely you mean *Hartbeat*.

Dame Heart *failure*, actually! (*She guffaws and nudges him again*)

Nick (*sternly*) Now then, madam, stop wasting police time, and tell us what it is you want!

Dame Oo! You're so masterful! (*She plays with the buttons on his tunic*) Well, I've come to beg a teensy weensy, itsy bitsy favour.

Nick What?

Dame I want to visit Billy Bumpkin.

Nick Billy Bumpkin? You mean Dick Turpin, don't you?

Dame (*giving him a playful push*) Oh, 'e's not Dick Turpin! 'E's not even Betty Turpin! It's all a mistake! The nearest 'e's ever been to armed robbery was in the highwayman ward at the maternity hospital!

Nab Highwayman ward?

Dame Yes! They'd run out of beds so 'is mum 'ad to—stand and deliver!

She and Nab hoot with laughter

Nick (*annoyed*) Madam! Stop wasting our time!

Dame Steady on! Don't get yer truncheon in a tremble! Can I see him now?

Nick No! He's been incarcerated!

Dame (*with great anguish*) Oo! Painful! (*To the audience*) The unkindest cut of all!

Nick He's not allowed any visitors.

Dame But I'm not just any old visitor! I'm all 'e 'as! (*She clings to Nick and pleads dramatically*) Oo! Please! Please? I beg you! You must let me see the poor unfortunate boy! I cannot bear the thought of him all alone in that deep, dark, damp, dank, dirty dismal dungeon! (*She cries on his shoulder*)

Nab cries on his other shoulder

Nab (*wailing*) Oow! Let her see him! Pleeease! I can't stand it!

Nick (*pushing them off*) Ger off! (*To the Dame*) All right! Just a short visit.

Dame (*all misery gone*) Ta! (*She starts towards the jail side*)

Nick (*stopping her*) Just a minute! What's in the bag?

Dame (*playing the innocent*) Bag? What bag? Oh, *this* bag! Nothin'
much... (*She makes for the exit*)

Nick stops her

Nick Madam, before you can see the prisoner I must ask you to show me
the contents of that bag!

*Nervously, she hands him the bag. He places it on the ground and reaches
inside. He takes out a large cake with a big red candle in the middle*

Dame (*laughing nervously*) 'E... 'e's got a very sweet tooth...

*Nick examines the candle. It comes loose and he pulls it from the cake—
the bottom part is a file! She tries to laugh it off*

   Oh! I've been lookin' for that everywhere! It's for... (*She mimes filing
   her nails*)

*Nick gives Nab the cake and file. He reaches into the bag and brings out
a large pair of pliers*

   That's mine! For... (*She mimes plucking her eyebrows*)

Nick gives Nab the pliers, and takes a big stick of dynamite from the bag

   Mine again! For... (*She mimes using a lipstick*)

*Nick gives Nab the dynamite, and takes from the bag a hacksaw. Dame
Dollop is about to speak*

Nick Don't tell me! You use this for cuttin' your toenails?! (*He gives the
saw to Nab*) All this looks highly suspicious, madam! A body search is
now called for!
Dame (*looking in the bag*) Oh, I don't think you'll find one of those in
there!
Nick *You*, madam! We're gonna search you!

*Slowly Dame Dollop backs away as Nick advances on her. Nab quickly
puts all the items back in the bag and clears it to the side*

Dame (*as she backs away*) Er... No...! I've changed me mind... I don't want to see him now... Oo!

Nick seizes hold of her. Comic business and ad libs as he and Nab give her a body search. Nick finds the end of a rope ladder which is coiled around the Dame's waist and hitherto concealed under her costume. He pulls the ladder and she spins away to the other side like a top. A tug of war ensues. Eventually, they succeed in hauling her across to their side

Nick (*holding up the ladder*) And what is this?!
Dame Oh! Is a woman to have no secrets! If you must know, it's my new wonder bra! They're all the rage! (*To someone in the audience*) You've got one on, haven't you, dear?
Nick (*throwing the ladder at her*) No visitors! And think yourself lucky I'm not arresting you for *acting suspicious*!

Nick marches off, jail side

Nab (*following, but giving her a parting shot*) Or tryin' to *act* at all!

Nab exits

Dame Dollop puts the ladder in the bag

Katie rushes on from the street side. Dick strolls on behind her

Katie Missus! Will they let you see 'im?!
Dame Nope! I was rumbled! They discovered a ladder in me tights! Still, it was worth a try.
Katie (*starting to howl*) Ooo! Billy! My Billy! Wahh!

She clings to Dame Dollop

Dame I can't understand you, Katie. For ages you've treated Billy as a joke, an' now you're cryin' buckets over 'im!
Katie (*between sobs*) Thas 'cos oi didn't know who 'e *really* was!
Dame Oh, don't say you think 'e's Dick Turpin as well! You know 'e's too thick to be anyone but Silly Billy!
Katie (*wailing*) Oo! Billy! 'E said 'e loved oi! Jus' think of the time oi've

wasted! Oi could 'ave bin in the arms o' Dick Turpin years ago! An' now 'e's gonna be 'anged! Oo! Wahh!

Wailing, Katie runs out, street side

Dame (*picking up the bag*) Oh, dear! I'm afraid things do look black for our Billy.

Dick Don't worry, Missus. The trial tomorrow will prove it's a mistake.

Dame Well, let's keep our fingers and everythin' else crossed. (*She moves to the street side exit*) I'd better go to Katie, she'll need the comfort of an *older* woman at a time like this. (*Parting shot to the audience*) I'll see if I can find one on the way!

The Dame exits

Dick (*to the audience, as himself*) I fear she is right. Things do look black for Billy. But worry not, my friends! I will not allow an innocent man to suffer on my account. See you at the trial! Adieu!

With a wave, Dick strides off

The Lights fade to Black-out

SCENE 3

The Courtroom

UC, *on a raised platform, is the judge's bench with a chair, judicial coat of arms, etc. Below it, to one side, is a low dais that serves as the dock. Benches set right and left. Entrances* R *and* L. *The backcloth and wings show sombre panelling and high windows*

Lord Lotaloot and Caroline are discovered seated together on a front bench R *and looking very solemn. Lotaloot has an enormous bandage around his foot*

Almost at once, bright music strikes up, and the farmhands, children and dancers make their noisy entrance. They obviously intend to treat the trial as a jolly day out rather than a serious occasion. Some carry picnic hampers, camping stools, etc. A few of the dancers carry trays with ice creams, hot dogs, drinks, etc. They go straight into a lively song and dance, much to the annoyance of Lotaloot who gets his foot trodden on a couple of times

Song 5

After the number, uproar breaks out. Some fight for the best seats. The children run riot and start climbing on to the bench. The sellers shout their wares. Pandemonium

Nick and Nab rush on from L. *Nick tries to bring order, while Nab tries to buy an ice cream*

Nick (*shouting above the din*) Silence in court! Silence! Oy! Stop that! Get down from there! Order! Order! (*He pulls out his whistle and blows it*)

All stop in mid action and go silent—all, except Nab

Nab (*yelling at the ice cream girl*) One raspberry ripple, please!
Nick (*pushing the sellers to the exit* R) Come on, you lot! Out! Where do you think you are! This is a courtroom, not (*local reference*)! Out!

The sellers exit

(*To the others*) Sit down! Sit down! The trial is about to commence! Sit down!

General hubbub as they all find seats and sit down

Be upstanding in court!

All rise with angry cries of "You've just told us to sit down!", "Make up your mind", etc., etc.

Silence in court! Silence for your judge—Mr Justice Mildew! (*He gestures dramatically towards the* L *entrance*)

All look in that direction with expectant awe, but no-one appears

Mr Justice Mildew!

They all look again

> *The Judge enters from* R. *He is very old, crusty and hard of hearing. He wears a long wig and red robe*

Judge (*calling to Nick*) Hey! You there!

All turn, see him and react. The Judge dodders over to Nick

You! Fishface! Where is the courtroom?

Nick (*dumbfounded*) You're in it, m'lud.

Judge In the *mud*?! What are you talking about?! (*He cups his ear*) Speak up!

Nick (*loudly and slowly*) You—are—in—court!

Judge I'm in port! (*He explodes*) How dare you! I haven't touched a drop since breakfast! Don't get above yourself, poopface! Is the fellow mad! I asked you a simple question! Where is the courtroom?! Bah! Don't bother! I'll find it meself!

He turns, and is about to dodder out the way he came in, when Lotaloot hobbles forward and intercepts him

Lotaloot (*bowing, stiffly*) Your servant, my Lord!

Judge (*snapping at him*) Who are you?! (*He sees the bandage*) And what are you doing with that baby on your foot?! I'll give you eighteen months for ill treating that child! You're nothing but a dastardly rogue, sir!

Lotaloot (*exploding*) What! You old...

Caroline (*quickly coming between them*) Gentlemen, kindly think of your blood pressure.

Judge (*on seeing her, his manner changes completely!*) Oh! I say! Who are you, my dear?

Caroline My name is Caroline and this is my father, Lord Lotaloot.

Judge (*looking from her to Lotaloot and shaking his head*) Impossible! How could something like *that* be responsible for something like *this*! Perhaps you can help me, my dear. I'm looking for the courtroom.

Caroline This *is* the courtroom, my Lord.

Judge (*looking about him*) Eh...? Why, so it is! (*He takes her hand and*

28   Dick Turpin
pats it) Oh, what a clever, resourceful and (*he eyes her cleavage*)—"up together" little lady you are!

Caroline returns to her father. The Judge dodders up to his bench. He bows to right and left, then goes to sit down. He misses the chair and falls out of sight. Roars of laughter from the crowd. He reappears with his wig awry. He sorts himself out and sits down. With a sigh of relief, everyone sits

Nab exits L

(*To Nick*) Well, get on with it, Fishface! Let the trial begin! (*He bangs his gavel*)
Nick (*calling to off* L) Bring in the prisoner!

From off L, *the cry of "Bring in the prisoner!" is repeated four times at varying distances*

A slight pause, then Nab's head appears from L

Nab What did you say?
All (*yelling at him*) Bring on the prisoner!

Nab goes, to reappear immediately, hauling on a long rope. Eventually, we see that Billy is secured to the other end of it. He is trussed up with huge chains and manacles. There is an enormous ball and chain around one ankle. He can hardly move, looks scared to death and on the verge of tears

"Oh"s and "Ah"s from the crowd. Nick and Nab manoeuvre Billy across and place him in the dock

Judge Read the charge!
Nick Yes, m'lud! (*With a flourish, he takes out a long scroll. He holds it up, and lets the other end drop to the ground with a thud. He starts to read*) Dick Turpin, you stand charged——
Judge (*banging the gavel*) Just a minute! Do you intend to read *all* of that?
Nick Yes, m'lud!
Judge Well, I for one haven't got that many years to waste! Just get to the nitty gritty!

Nick Yes, m'lud. (*He reads*) Dick Turpin, you stand charged of the awful and very naughty crime of highway robbery! Er... (*He quickly goes through the rest of the scroll*) Bla! Bla! Bla! Waffle! Waffle! Bla! Bla! Full stop! (*He quickly rolls up the scroll, then turns to Billy*) How say you, Dick Turpin? Do you plead guilty or not guilty?

Billy (*pleading*) Oi *baint* Dick Turpin! (*To the others*) Tell 'em oi baint! (*To the audience*) Folks! You tell 'em! Oi'm not Dick Turpin, am oi?!

"No!" from the audience. Nick leads them into "Oh yes, he is!", "Oh no, he isn't!" routine. Uproar from the crowd. The Judge yells for order and bangs his gavel

Judge Silence! (*To all, including the audience*) Any further disturbance and I shall clear the court! Now! Who speaks for the defence?

Dame (*calling, off* R) I do! I do!

Dame Dollop sails on from R, *wearing an outrageous version of a barrister's garb and carries a large bundle of legal papers. She strikes a pose*

Tra la! Never fear, Dollop's 'ere! The Rumpole of (*local place*)! (*She goes to the bench*) Mornin', Judge! Love the hair-do! Is that the latest from (*local hairdressers*)?

Judge So, you are the council for the defence, eh?

Dame I is, your warship!

Judge I've never seen you in the high courts.

Dame And you never will! I can't wear 'em! Not with my bunions!

Judge Have you been at the bar long?

Dame Since openin' time! Does it show?

Judge Enough of this tomfoolery! (*He bangs his gavel*)

Dame 'Ere! That's handy! I wish I'd brought some nuts with me!

Judge (*yelling at her*) Get on with the trial!

Dame All right! All right! Don't get yer perm in a pickle! (*To the audience*) Members of the jury, you see before you a pitiful creature! (*She goes up and gestures dramatically towards Billy*) He is the victim of a gross misunderstanding! He is the result of a bit of harmless fun that went horribly wrong!

Billy 'Ere!' Don't you bring my mum and dad into this!

Dame I put it to you, members of the jury, could this gormless twit be anyone but Silly Billy Bumpkin! I thank you! (*She bows*)

The crowd clap wildly. The Judge bangs his gavel, and Nick yells "Silence in court"

I call my first witness. A young lady who has known the accused for many years. I call—Miss Daisy Cowslip!

To suitable music, Daisy trots on from R

The crowd cheer. Daisy curtsies and the music stops

Judge (*outraged*) I don't believe it! What is the meaning of this! Are you asking this court to listen to the evidence of a … a common cow?!

Daisy reacts to this

Dame (*going to Daisy*) Oh! Now you've gone and 'urt 'er feelin's! Daisy's not common, are you love?

Daisy shakes her head

No! She's as well brung up as wot you is! (*To the audience*) You want to 'ear what Daisy's got to say, don't you, members of the jury?

"Yes" from the audience

Good! Now, Daisy, I'm goin' to ask you some questions. Is that all right?

Daisy nods her head

Do you know a Billy Bumpkin?

Daisy nods her head

Do you see 'im in this court?

Daisy looks around. She sees Billy, trots up, and nestles against him affectionately. Dame Dollop goes up and starts to lead Daisy back down stage

Have you ever known him to be anyone *other* than Billy Bumpkin?

Judge You are leading the witness!

Dame (*literally doing so*) She's used to it! (*To Daisy*) 'Ave you?

Daisy (*shaking her head*) Mooo!

Dame 'E's not Dick Turpin, is 'e?

Daisy (*shaking her head, vigorously*) Mooo!

Dame (*to all, triumphantly*) There!

The crowd clap and cheer. Dame Dollop and Daisy curtsy. The Judge bangs his gavel

Judge (*fuming*) Never in all my years on the bench have I witnessed such a ridiculous display! It's all balderdash and tripe!

Daisy reacts, and starts trembling all over

Dame (*rushing to comfort her*) Oh no! You shouldn't of mentioned that word!

Judge What word?

Dame Tripe!

Daisy panics and runs up and down, mooing loudly, and kicking her legs out. Uproar from the crowd. Dame Dollop manages to calm her down, and leads her to the exit R

You go back to your nice field, Daisy dear, and try to forget all about it. It's my fault. I shouldn't 'ave brought you 'ere! I'm just a silly old...

Daisy Mooooo!

Dame That's right! Off you go!

Daisy trots out R

(*To the Judge*) She'll be off colour for days now! I won't get as much as a Milky Way out of her!

Judge Have you any more *so-called* witnesses? A herd of elephants perhaps?

Dame (*ignoring his sarcasm*) Just one. I call—Katie Cuddlesome!

Katie enters from R, weeping as usual. She runs straight to Billy and throws her arms around him

Katie Oo! Dick…! My hero…! Oh, what 'ave they done to you…! Ooo…!
Judge (*to Nab*) Remove that person from the prisoner!

Nab prises Katie away from Billy and gets kicked on the shin for his trouble

Dame Do you know a Billy Bumpkin?
Katie (*hesitatingly*) Wull, oi…
Judge (*snapping*) Answer the question!
Katie Oi knows someone who *calls* 'imself that, but 'e be really…
Dame (*clamping her hand over Katie's mouth*) Oh! There was a great big bee just about to fly into your gob! (*She pulls Katie aside and whispers to her*) Don't tell 'em who you *think* 'e is! You'll ruin everythin'! Jus' say 'e's Billy Bumpkin!
Katie (*pushing Dame Dollop away and declaring dramatically to the world*) Never! The truth mus' be known! 'E *is* Dick Turpin! (*She rushes to Billy*) 'E told oi so 'imself! And we loves each other! (*She throws her arms around him*) Oh, Dick!
Billy Oh, heck!
Dame Oh, B—blow!

Uproar from the crowd. The Judge bangs the gavel and silence falls

Judge (*sternly*)　　　'Tis all too plain this man is a sinner!
　　　　　　　　　　I've heard enough, and it's time for dinner!
　　　　　　　　　　For all the vile crimes he has carried out,
　　　　　　　　　　I find Turpin guilty beyond a shadow of doubt!
　　　　　　　　　　(*He puts on his black cap*)
　　　　　　　　　　Take him to the gallows with solemn tread,
　　　　　　　　　　And hang him by the neck until he be—*dead*!

Sensational uproar! Nick and Nab try to pull Billy out L, with Katie still clinging to him

Dick suddenly appears DR. (See Production Notes) He wears the cloak and mask etc., and carries two pistols. He fires one into the air as he enters

All noise and movement stop. Dick quickly stuffs the used pistol into his belt and strides to C

Dick Release that man! He is innocent! (*He points the loaded pistol at Nick and Nab*) Release him, I say!

Terrified, they let go of Billy and run out L

Judge How dare you burst into my courtroom! Who are you?!
Dick I am— (*he strikes a swashbuckling pose*) Dick Turpin!

Reaction from all

Judge But I've just sentenced Dick Turpin to be hanged!
Dick (*indicating Billy; with a hearty laugh*) What, *that* poor fellow? Ha ha ha! I will prove to you that *I* am the one and only Dick Turpin, Prince of Highwaymen! (*He moves to Lotaloot and bows to him*) Sir! Was not your coach held up but yesterday?
Lotaloot It was!
Dick And were you not relieved of two guineas?
Lotaloot I was!
Dick (*whipping out a pouch and tossing it to Lotaloot*) And is this not the purse that contained those guineas?
Lotaloot (*after a quick examination*) It is! Egad...! He *is* Dick Turpin!

Reaction from all. Katie lets go of Billy and gazes open-mouthed at Dick

Dick (*to the dumbstruck Judge*) Case proven I think, m'lud! (*To all*) And now I will trespass no further on your time. The broad highway beckons and I must be gone! (*He goes to Caroline and bows elegantly*) Dearest lady, your servant.

At this, Katie gives a strangled squeak. Dick strides to DR, *and turns*

Farewell!

Dick fires the pistol into the air, and dashes out R

Katie (*awestruck, and taking a few steps over*) Dick Turpin... Oh, my 'ero!
Billy (*shuffling to her*) Katie...
Katie (*turning and snapping at him*) Oh, go away, you ... you Bumpkin, you!

Wailing, Katie runs out DR

Billy (*to the audience*) Women!
Dame Well, Judge Dredd, is my client free to leave the court?
Judge Bah! You can *all* leave! Get out! Case dismissed! (*He bangs his gavel for the last time*)
All Hurray!

Song 6

The Judge exits at the back

The others burst into song, surge forward and surround Billy. He is hastily striped of his chains and hoisted on to the shoulders of some of the men. They parade him around. On the last note of music they form a tableau, and the Lights fade to Black-out

SCENE 4

Outside the Jail

Tabs, or the frontcloth used in Act I, Scene 2

The Lighting is dark and mysterious. "Villain" music

Smash and Grab, two villainous-looking ruffians, creep on from L, *and look about. Satisfied the coast is clear, they signal to someone off* L

A tall, sinister figure sweeps on. It is—Mr X! He wears a full head mask with just eyes and mouth visible. (See Costume Notes) He moves between Smash and Grab

Mr X (*his voice is deep and menacing*) Are we alone?
Smash (*grovelling*) Aye, Mr X!
Grab (*likewise*) Aye! The coast is clear!
Mr X I think not! What about— (*he points to the audience*) them!

Smash and Grab see the audience, react, and make to scuttle off. Mr X grabs them and gives a mocking laugh

Ha ha ha! Stay where you are, blockheads! We have nothing to fear from these pathetic, puny plebs! (*Directly to the audience*) Listen, morons, you are in the presence of royalty! You see before you—the King of Crime! Ha ha ha! The secret of my success is my amazing ability to put the blame on other criminals. For instance, since moving into this neighbourhood all my crimes have been put down to a local highwayman. A young upstart called Dick Turpin. Ha ha ha! Clever, eh? Don't you think I'm clever? (*By-play with the audience*)

Smash Wot's next on the agenda, Mr X? Is it another horphanage to rob an' burn to the ground?

Grab Or is it another lonely old widder to beat up, and rob of 'er life savin's?

Both laugh with horrible villainy, then Smash gets an idea

Smash 'Ere! I've just 'ad a fought!

Mr X A miracle! Well, what is it?

Smash (*in loud stage whisper, and indicating the audience*) All *that* lot ain't at 'ome, are they? Why don't we nip round to their 'ouses an' burgle 'em!

Grab (*rubbing his hands with devilish glee*) Aye!

Mr X (*after contemplating the audience*) Pah! T'would be a waste of time! By the look of them they haven't got anything worth pinching! And they've been robbed of their brains already by the look of it! Ha ha ha!

Smash (*looking off* R, *and panicking*) Mr X! Someone's comin' this way!

Mr X Then let us be gone! And I will try to think of yet another dastardly crime that can be blamed on Dick Turpin! Ha ha ha!

Laughing their evil laughs, and snarling at the audience, they exit L

The Lighting becomes bright

Katie flounces on from R, *with Billy hot on her heels*

Katie (*turning and snapping at him*) Oh, go away! Stop followin' oi about!

Billy But, Katie...

Katie If you don't leave oi alone, oi'll ... oi'll throw you in the duck pond!

Billy You didn't say that when you thought oi were Dick Turpin!

Katie Well, you *baint* Dick Turpin! You'm jus' silly old Billy Bumpkin!

Billy (*moving to her*) Oh, Katie, my little sugar plum!

Katie (*pushing him away*) Keep away from oi! (*She stomps to the exit* L)

Dick enters L. *He is now back in rustic attire*

Katie bumps into him

(*To Dick*) An' you can get out of the way, an' all!

Katie exits

Dick (*amused, then moving to Billy*) Hullo, Billy! Oi've just 'eard the good news about your release this marnin'.

Billy (*all gloom and doom*) Huh! A fat lot o' good 'tis done oi! Katie won't 'ave nothin' to do wi' oi again!

Dick Cheer up! Oi'm sure she'll come round in time.

Billy Ar! But oi'll be too old to do anythin' about it then! (*Gloomily, he slouches to the exit* R) Oi be so depressed, oi've a good mind to emigrate to (*nearby town or village*)!

Billy exits

Laughing to himself, Dick watches him go

Caroline enters from L. *She regards Dick for a moment, then approaches him*

Caroline Good afternoon, Master Appleseed.

Dick (*turning*) What...? Oh! (*On seeing her, he forgets himself*) Good afternoon. You remember me? Er... (*He hastily assumes his accent*) You remember oi?

Caroline But of course I do. You were so gallant and helpful yesterday at Dame Dollop's farm. I ... er ... seem to remember that you kissed my hand. (*She offers her hand to him*)

Dick (*taking it and gazing into her eyes*) Did oi? What, like this? (*He kisses her hand*)

Lord Lotaloot hobbles on from R, *still with his foot bandaged. He reacts at the couple*

Lotaloot (*coughing with disapproval*) Ah hum!

Caroline gives a start and looks towards her father. Dick continues with the hand kissing

Caroline Father ... er ... You remember Master Appleseed from Dollop's farm?
Lotaloot (*with a sniff*) Indeed I do! The fellow with the built-in manicure set!

Caroline gently extracts her hand. Dick sees Lotaloot and gives him a rather embarassed bow

Caroline (*to Dick*) As a matter of fact, we are on our way to the farm now.
Dick (*gazing at her, and forgetting himself again*) Really? How lovely ... er ... (*With the accent*) Oh, be 'ee?
Caroline Yes. You may not be aware of it, but tomorrow is my coming of age.
Dick Congratulations! (*He takes her hand and starts kissing it again*)
Lotaloot That means she's now old enough to wash her own hands!

Dick drops her hand

Caroline Tomorrow evening we will be holding a grand party at Lotaloot Hall to celebrate my birthday. My father wishes to invite everyone at the farm. He feels it is the least he can do after that unfortunate misunderstanding with poor Billy Bumpkin. Don't you, Father dear?
Lotaloot (*blustering and eager to dismiss the subject*) Well ... er ... Yes! yes! (*He hobbles across to the exit* R) Now let us be about the business and return home. This accursed foot is on fire again! Come, Caroline!

Lotaloot exits

Caroline I hope that you will be able to attend my party, Master Appleseed.
Dick (*completely forgetting himself now*) Oh, I would fly to the furthest star, climb the highest peak, and swim the widest ocean to be at your party!
Caroline (*moved, and not a little surprised*) My! You are extremely eloquent for a farm labourer!

Dick (*hastily assuming his accent*) Oh, ar! Well, 'tis amazin' what you can pick up from *Farmers' Weekly*. Allow oi to escort you to the farm.
Caroline Many thanks. (*She offers her hand*)

He takes it and starts kissing it again

Lotaloot hobbles back on from R

Lotaloot Gadzooks! He's at it again!

The couple part

Come, Caroline! Don't keep me waiting! (*Impatiently, he stamps his bad foot, then hops about in agony*)

Surpressing their laughter, Dick and Caroline hurry out R. *Lotaloot limps painfully out after them*

The Lighting becomes dark and mysterious. "Villain" music

Mr X creeps on from L, *followed by Smash and Grab. Mr X is laughing and rubbing his hands with devilish glee*

Mr X Well, my faithful fellons, that solves our problem of finding another crime to commit!
Smash Wot d'you mean, Mr X?
Mr X Didn't you hear? We are going to a birthday party at Lotaloot Hall tomorrow night!
Grab (*dumbly*) But, Mr X, we ain't bin invited.
Mr X Numbskull! Since when have we had to wait for an invitation to go into someone's house? (*Ruminating*) Yes, Lotaloot Hall. I can't understand why I never thought of breaking into that place before. (*To the audience, with much menace*) And if any of you breath a word about this, you'll wish you had never been born! (*By-play with the audience, then to the two rogues*) Come, my gruesome twosome! Let us return to our hide-out and make plans. Just think of it— (*with mock horror*) a robbery at Lotaloot Hall! How terrible! Another awful crime committed by that dreadful Dick Turpin! Ha ha ha!

Laughing their evil laughs, they exit L, *amid boos and hisses*

The Lights fade to Black-out

SCENE 5

The Kitchen at Dollop's Farm

The backcloth and wings show beam and plaster walls, a large kitchen range, a dresser with china, pots and pans, a sink under the window, sacks of animal feed, etc. Entrances R and L

Katie, Daisy, the farmhands and the dancers are discovered. The junior dancers as various farm animals. They go straight into a song and dance

Song 7

After the applause, Dame Dollop rushes on from L

Dame (*as she enters*) Oy oy oy! What's all the row about?! 'Ere! What are you lot doin' in my nice, clean fitted kitchen! (*She shoos them out R*) Out you go! Go on! Shoo! Get back to work! Out!

They have all gone except for Daisy who is "hiding" behind the Dame

(*To the audience*) Have they all gone?

"No!" from the audience

Who's still 'ere?

"Daisy!" from the audience

Where is she?

"She's behind you!" routine with Dame Dollop turning and Daisy keeping behind her. Eventually they come face to face. Dame Dollop jumps with fright and falls over. Daisy frisks about

Ohhh! (*She gets up*) Oh, you mischievious milk machine, you! Come on, out you go! (*She pushes Daisy towards the exit R*)

As the cow goes out, Dame Dollop realizes she is holding her tail

An' take yer rear screen wiper with ya! Animals in my kitchen indeed! (*To someone in the audience*) I bet you don't 'ave animals in *your* kitchen, missus. (*She peers closer*) Sorry, my mistake! I can see you probably do! Guess what, folks! I've been invited to a super party tomorrow night at Lotaloot 'all! Ooo! I'm really lookin' forward to it! It'll give me a chance to wear that little number I got from Chelsea Girl! (*To someone*) I said Chelsea *girl*—not Chelsea *pensioner*!

Billy (*off* R; *calling*) Katie! Come 'ere!
Dame Oh, look out! 'Ere comes (*topical romantic couple*) again!

Katie stomps on from R, *carrying a round sieve. Billy is hot on her heels. She makes straight for exit* L

Billy Katie! Listen to oi…!

Katie stops, turns and breaks the sieve over his head, then marches out L

Dame Sorry, you've been framed! (*Laughing, she removes the sieve and tosses it off stage*)

Billy looks very dejected

Oh, come on, Billy, cheer up! Just think about that smashin' party we're all goin' to!
Billy Oi can't think about anythin' but Katie! (*Very serious*) Do you know, when oi baint thinkin' of 'er, my mind be a complete blank.
Dame (*to the audience*) There! I bet that came as a big surprise to you all!

Nick and Nab march on from R. *They do their knee bending routine*

Nick
Nab } (*together*) Evenin' all!
Dame I 'ope you two 'aven't come 'ere again to arrest Billy for bein' someone 'e ain't! I can definitely say he is *not* Lord Lucan!

Billy just stares blankly into space

Nick What's up with him?

Dame E's in love, but 'e's 'ad 'is 'opes crushed!
Nab (*squirming*) Ooo! Painful!
Dame Not even the thought of goin' to the party at the 'all cheers him up.
Nick (*indicating Billy*) I hope *he* behaves himself while he's there.
Dame Oh, 'e's house trained!
Nick Well, it's going to be a real slap up do! Fifteen courses of fancy food!
And he looks like he'd drink his soup with a fork!
Nab An' everyone knows you use a knife.

_____

Optional Slapstick Scene

They give him a look

Dame (*to Nick, after weighing up Billy*) Yes, you're right! 'E's such an
uncouth youth! (*Ultra posh*) Hi don't want 'im showin' me hup hinfront
of hall those posh persons! I think I'd better give 'im some lessons in
table manners. You two can 'elp!

*A slapstick routine follows in which the Dame, with the help and hin-
drance of Nick and Nab, instructs Billy in the art of table manners and
etiquette. Nick and Nab can fetch a table and the necessary props from off
stage. See Production Notes*

When it is over, Nick and Nab exit, taking the table etc. with them

_____

Dick and Parson Goodfellow enter from R

Katie and the farmhands enter from L

Dick 'Ello, Dame Dollop! Oi've brought you a visitor.
Dame (*excited*) Oh! Who is it?
Parson (*stepping into view*) It's me, Dame Dollop.
Dame (*to the audience, disappointed*) Oh no! (*To Parson*) What can I do
for you, Rev?
Parson I have a small request.
Dame Well, none of us are perfect!
Parson I have just received an invitation to the party at Lotaloot Hall

tomorrow. I ... er ... (*Moving nearer to her*) I... I was wondering... (*He moves even nearer*) Dear Dame Dollop...

Dame (*quick aside to the audience*) Look out! 'E's after something!

Parson It would give me enormous pleasure...

Dame I bet it would!

Parson If you would allow me to be your escort.

Dame An *escort*! Couldn't you be a BMW?! (*She guffaws and gives him a playful push*) Oh, all right! Seein' as how (*popular heart throb*) ain't around, I'll let you take me.

Parson (*clasping his hands with sheer delight*) Oh, thank you! Heaven be praised!

Parson skips out R

Dame (*to the audience*) See the effect I 'ave on men! I drive 'em crazy!

Dick Oi can't wait to get to that party, can you?

Dame Boy, I'm as good as there already!

Song 8

A lively song and dance involving everyone. Even Daisy and the animals can enter and join in. Billy tries to approach Katie, but gets the cold shoulder. On the last note of the music——

——the CURTAIN *falls*

ACT II

The Ballroom of Lotaloot Hall

An elegant room of the period, with long, gilt framed mirrors, portraits and hanging chandeliers. L are tall french windows leading to a moonlit garden. R are double doors or an archway leading to other rooms. Back C is a large fireplace. This later swings open to reveal a secret passage. Up in the L corner stands a folding screen. A few gilt chairs are set against the walls down stage

The farmhands, children and other guests are discovered grouped about the stage. Dick and Caroline are leading the dancers in a stately gavotte, accompanied by singing. Dick and the farmhands are in their "Sunday best", while the other guests are more elegantly attired

Song 9

After the number, the dancers bow and curtsy to each other, then disperse up stage

Katie runs on from R, and straight out through the windows L

A split second later, Billy enters R, and runs out after her, calling "Katie! Come back 'ere!"

This has apparantly been going on all evening and none of the others take any notice

Lord Lotaloot enters from R, with Nick and Nab. They have him squashed between them, and he finds this very annoying. Comic business as he tries to move about with them sticking to him like glue

Lotaloot (*squirming betweem them*) Bah! Aren't you carrying this security business a bit too far! Egad! I feel like a sardine!

Nick We are only doin' our duty, m'lud.

They do their knee bending routine a few times. Lotaloot is forced to bend with them and they bump him with their knees. He also gets his bad foot trodden on

Lotaloot Ooo! Gadzooks! I'll tolerate this lunacy no longer! Get away from me! (*He pushes them away*) Go somewhere else and play bookends!

They move to DL

Katie runs on from L, *and straight out* R. *Billy is hot on her heels. En route he treads on Lotaloot's foot*

Lotaloot hops about in agony, then spots Caroline chatting with Dick

(*Summoning her*) Caroline!

Caroline (*coming down to him*) Yes, Father?

Lotaloot (*taking her to one side, sternly*) My child, you seem to be spending all your time in the company of that young farm fellow!

Caroline Do you mean Dick Appleseed, Father?

Lotaloot Surely the conversation of a farm labourer can't be that fascinating?

Caroline Oh, but it *is*! (*She teases him*) He's offered to show me how his dibber works.

Lotaloot (*exploding*) His *what*!

Caroline For planting potatoes.

Lotaloot (*blustering*) Oh—er—well, don't be neglecting your other guests! That reminds me... (*He looks about*) Where is Dame Dollop and Parson Goodfellow? Zounds! I hope they haven't discovered one of the secret passages! We might never see them again!

Dame (*off* R; *calling*) Yooo! Hooo!

Nick (*to Lotaloot*) You spoke too soon!

Dame Dollop sails on from R. *She wears an outrageous version of an eighteenth century ball gown, a tall white wig, etc.*

Dame (*exuberantly, as she enters*) Never fear, Dollop's 'ere! The life an' soul of the party is back!

Katie runs on from R, *and straight out* L. *Billy follows. He is now showing signs of fatigue*

(*To the audience*) Hi folks! What do you think of the outfit? (*She does a twirl*) I feel like a cross between Madonna and Mr Whippy! Don't you think it really does somethin' for me? (*She invites audience response*) Well, I may look absolutely gorgeous, but I 'aven't 'ad a single offer all flippin' night! (*To someone*) Of a *dance*, you mucky pup! Oo! The minds of some people! (*To the others*) Now then, boys, which of you lucky lads is goin' to sweep me off me feet?

Nab Sorry, but I haven't brought my crane with me!

Dame (*sidling up to Lotaloot*) How about you, your 'ardship? I bet you can't wait to get me on the floor!

Lotaloot (*blustering*) Er... I ... I'd love to...

Dame (*holding out her arms to him*) Come on, then! Let's boogie, baby!

Lotaloot (*hastily retreating behind Caroline*) No ... no, really, I...

Dame (*in a huff*) Oh, please yerself! (*To the audience*) Good innit! 'Ere I am, the belle of the ball, an' no-one wants to pull me!

Song 10 *(optional)*

A comedy song for everyone, led by Dame Dollop. Comic antics with her and Nick and Nab. The audience can be involved if desired

Lotaloot (*to all*) Dear friends, I trust that you have enjoyed the proceedings thus far?

Cries of "Oh yes!", "Thank you!", "Very nice", etc

Good! Good! Now, I have a special treat in store for you all! Later on, I will be showing you my *pièce de résistance*!

Dame (*to the audience*) I should send the kids home now!

Lotaloot As a fitting finale to such a splendid evening, I have arranged—at no little expense—a magnificent firework display to take place in the gardens!

"Oohs" and "ahhs" from everyone

Until then, let the party continue! There is still food aplenty in the banqueting hall, so if you would care to...

Dame Grub's up! (*She pushes her way through*) Gangway! Gangway!

Dame Dollop rushes out R

The farmfolk exit hot on her heels. The other guests exit more sedately. Dick and Caroline exit

Nick and Nab get on either side of Lotaloot. They squash him up and do a comic exit R

Slight pause, then Katie runs on from L, *and straight out* R

Billy staggers on from L, *utterly exhausted. He drops to his knees, and crawls over to one of the chairs* R

Billy (*to the audience, hauling himself on to the chair*) Phew! Talk about givin' oi the run around! Lindford Christy'd 'ave a job to keep up wi' 'er! Phew! (*He puts his head in his hands*)

Two or three loud taps are heard coming from behind the back wall

(*Reacting*) Wot were that?!

The sounds are repeated. Billy gets up and moves C

T—there 'tis again! (*To the audience, getting scared*) D—d—did you hear it, folks?

"Yes!" from the audience

Ooo! 'Tis p—proper s—spooky! Oi … oi bet this place be 'aunted!

The sounds are repeated. He gulps, trembles and darts terrified glances about the room

Oo! Mother!

The sounds are repeated, louder

Ahhh! T—t—tis a g—g—ghost! (*He covers his eyes, and stands there shaking all over and moaning*)

Dame Dollop enters from R. *She is holding a huge prop chicken drumstick. She reacts at the sight of Billy, grins mischieviously at the audience, and creeps over to him. She taps him on on the shoulder*

He yells, and leaps about four feet in the air! Dame Dollop laughs

Oh, missus! Oi thought you was the ghost, come to get oi!
Dame Ghost?! You big soft nellie! There's no such things as ghosts! They are just pigments of the imagination!
Billy But oi *'eard* it! (*He indicates the audience*) They 'eard it as well! Din ya, folks?

"Yes!" from the audience

Dame (*to them*) Yah! You lot 'ave been watchin' too many *X Files!*
Billy (*scared*) It were a weird—eerie sound! A spooky tappin' sort o' noise!

Three loud taps are heard

Dame (*unconcerned*) What, like that?
Billy Ar! Like that… (*He suddenly panics and clings to the Dame*) Ahh! The ghost! 'Tis 'ere! 'Elp! Save oi!
Dame (*disentangling herself from him*) Ger off! You soppy great twerp! That ain't no ghost! It sounds like bad plumbin' to me!

The sounds are repeated. She looks upstage

It came from up 'ere! (*She goes up to the* R *corner of the back wall*)

Billy follows nervously behind her. She listens

It's stopped now!

The sounds of slow, heavy footsteps are now heard behind the back wall. Comic business as they put their ears to the wall, and follow the progress of the footsteps towards the fireplace, where they stop. Dame Dollop and Billy move away to UL, *and get into a huddle. They converse in hushed tones*

Billy P—perhaps 'tis mice!

Dame If it is, they're wearin' Doc Martens! No, there's somebody behind that fireplace!

Billy Who d'you reckon 'tis?

Dame Well, it ain't Santa Claus, cos 'e's been already! (*Or*) 'E aint due yet! Shh! What's that?!

A metallic, clicking noise is heard from behind fireplace

The Lighting grows dark and mysterious. At the same time, low threatening music creeps in. Dame Dollop and Billy cling to each other in mute terror. There is a final loud click. Very slowly, the fireplace creaks open— to stage left. An eerie, greenish light spills through. Billy and the Dame are having silent hysterics! She runs behind the folding screen, dragging Billy with her. The music mounts as the fireplace opens up fully

Mr X emerges

Dramatic chords! He snarls at the audience. The music fades out. Mr X looks cautiously around the room, then closes up the fireplace. He moves to the windows L, *and gives a special low whistle. From off stage* L *the whistle is repeated*

Mr X moves back into the room, as Smash and Grab appear at the windows. Grab carries a large black bag with "swag" written on it in white

Mr X Come in! We are safe for the moment. They are all at the other end of the house, feeding their miserable faces!

Smash and Grab move into the room. They sneer at the audience

Smash (*rubbing his hands with eager anticipation*) Ready when you are, Mr X! Lead us to the booty!

Grab Aye! Do we start wiv the stuff in this 'ere room? (*He starts to open his bag*)

Mr X No! Listen carefully!

They go into an "evil" huddle

Later on tonight there is going to be a firework display in the garden...

Smash Oo! Thas nice!

Grab Yeah! Will there be any sparklers?

Smash (*getting carried away*) And Catherine wheels! I love Catherine wheels...

Mr X Silence, you blockheads! There isn't much time! Now, listen to me! Everyone will go outside to watch the display! That will be the time for us to carry out our business. It should not take us long. There is only *one* thing I wish to obtain. That old fool Lord Lotaloot has in his possession some jewels. They are worth far more than anything else in the entire household.

Smash Where are these jewels stashed?

Mr X That I have yet to find out. But fear not, I will soon ascertain their whereabouts. Now! Get back to the bushes and await my signal! Go!

Smash and Grab exit through the windows

Mr X gives the audience a snarl, then goes to the fireplace. He presses a certain part of the moulding and the fireplace creaks open

He gives the audience his evil laugh, and disappears inside

The fireplace creaks shut behind him. The Lighting returns to normal. Dame Dollop creeps out from behind one side of the screen, as Billy does the same from the other side. Comic business as they, back to back, creep slowly towards each other and eventually touch rears. Terrified, they slowly turn and come face to face. Both yell, then hug each other with relief

Dame Oh, Billy! What are we goin' to do?! Mr Nasty an' 'is cronies are goin' to rob 'is Lordship! We've got to do somethin'!

Billy (*running about like a headless chicken*) Don't panic! Don't panic! Don't panic!

Dame (*grabbing him*) Stop runnin' about like yer pants were on fire! What are we goin' to do?

Billy (*calming down*) Oi know wot we can do!

Dame What?

Billy We can—*panic*! (*He starts running about again*)

Dame (*grabbing him*) Come 'ere! Listen! Let's go an' warn the others!

Billy Oi've got a better idea. Let's go an' warn the others!

He rushes towards the exit R, followed by the Dame

   Katie enters

Billy bumps into her

Katie Oh! Not *you* again! (*She is about to turn on her heel*)

Billy pulls her back into the room

Billy Katie! Somethin' awful be goin' to 'appen!
Katie (*shaking him off*) Ar! It will, if you don't leave oi alone!
Dame Katie, you'll never believe what we... Oh, sit over there an' we'll
   show you what 'appened!

She sits Katie on one of the side chairs. Billy gets in position

   Now! It all started when I came in 'ere an' found Billy! Go!

*The following sequence should be accompanied by a recorded sound
effect of music taken at high speed. Suggestion: a 33 1/3 RPM record of
Khachaturian's* Sabre Dance *played at 45 RPM. If this is not practical,
suitable "hurry" music can be played on piano. Dame Dollop and Billy
do a comic "fast forward" reconstruction of all the action from the point
where she taps him on the shoulder, to where they come from behind the
screen and bump into each other. They even re-enact the parts of the three
villains. They do it in silence, except for when they supply their own sound
effects, such as the tapping sounds, the footsteps, the creaking fireplace
and Mr X's evil laugh. They* do not *make practical use of the fireplace. By
the end, they are both physical wrecks and have to hold each other up. The
music stops*

   (*To Katie, gasping*) There!
Katie (*rising, confused*) Er... Oi'm sorry ... would you mind repeatin'
   that.

*Billy and the Dame groan, and collapse in a heap on the floor. She drops
her chicken drumstick*

   Parson Goodfellow enters from R

Parson (*seeing them*) Goodness me! (*Going to them*) Dame Dollop! Billy! (*To Katie*) Are they unwell?

Katie (*moving over*) Oi dunno, Parson. They were tryin' to tell oi somethin', but...

They assist the Dame and Billy to their feet

Dame Oh, Parson! You'll never believe what we... It all started when I came in 'ere an' found Billy...

Billy (*jumping in quick*) No! Oi baint goin' through all that again! We over'eard three nasties plannin' to rob Lotaloot 'all tonight!

Dame An' they're gonna nick 'is Lordship's family jewels!

Katie and Parson react with horror

Parson (*moving away to* L) Heavens above! This is terrible! What are we going to do?

Katie We've got to tell the others at once!

She rushes towards the exit R, *followed by Billy and the Dame. Suddenly, the menacing voice of Mr X freezes them in their tracks! It comes from Parson Goodfellow! His physical bearing has changed a lot too*

Mr X Don't move! (*He draws a pistol*) Stay exactly where you are!

Dame That voice! It sounds like...

Billy The one they called—Mr X!

Mr X Turn around—slowly!

They do so. Thay are dumbfounded to see their Parson aiming a pistol at them

Katie (*finding her voice*) P—P—Parson...?

Mr X (*in his Parson voice*) Yes, my child? (*He whips off his hat with the white wig attached*)

The three gasp. Mr X gives his evil laugh. He replaces the hat. Billy is about to make a run for it

I said—*don't move!*

Billy freezes

Dame (*calling, very weakly*) H—h—help!
Mr X Silence, you flea-bitten old hag!
Dame 'Ere! Less of the old!
Mr X Stop your wagging tongue, or I will do it for you! (*He brandishes the pistol*)

Dame Dollop gulps loudly

Dick (*off* R; *calling*) Dame Dollop! Where are you?!

Mr X reacts at this

Dame Ha! Now you've 'ad it! The Cavalry's arrived!
Mr X (*pointing to the fireplace*) Get up there! (*He brandishes the pistol*) Move!

The frightened group scuttle up to the fireplace. Mr X joins them

Look the other way!

They all turn away. Keeping the pistol trained on their backs, Mr X presses the moulding and the fireplace creaks open

Turn around!

They do so

Get inside! (*He points to the aperture*)
Dame Ugh! Go in there! I bet there's spiders!
Mr X (*waving the pistol*) Get inside, I say! And I warn you, don't even think about trying to get away! Inside!

Quaking with fear, Billy goes inside. Katie follows

Dame Dollop bends to go in, then stops with her bottom sticking up

Dame (*to the audience*) Oh well, folks! Out of the fryin' pan, into the fire! (*She laughs weakly*)

Mr X jabs her bottom with his pistol

She yelps, and disappears from sight

Mr X gives the audience his laugh, and goes inside

The fireplace creaks shut behind him

Dick, Caroline, Lotaloot, Nick and Nab enter from R, *followed by all the guests*

Dick (*as they enter*) Katie! Billy! (*To the others*) No, they baint in 'ere either!

Lotaloot This is most perplexing!

Man Don't ee worry yerself, m'lud. Oi expect ole Dollop be gone somewhere to sleep it off!

Woman Ar! An' oi bet Billy Bumpkin be still chasin' Katie round the garden!

All laugh and agree

Nick (*very serious*) Well, I smell a rat!

Nab 'Ere! Don't look at me when you say that!

Nick My policeman's nose tells me there are suspicious circumstances here! I wonder what is afoot?

Nab It's the thing on the end of your leg!

Nick PC Nab! Get lookin' for clues! (*He whips out his magnifying glass*)

Nab goes down on all fours and searches the floor. He finds Dame Dollop's chicken drumstick, and, getting up, hands it to Nick

Nab Here you are, Hercule!

Nick (*holding it up*) A chicken leg!

Nab Go on, say it! You suspect—*foul* play! Ta ra!

Nick (*examining it through his glass*) Mm! Only one bite has been taken! What does that tell us?

Nab Too much garlic?

Caroline Dame Dollop was eating one of those when I last saw her.

Nick Ah ha! And she's certainly not the type to leave a chicken leg half eaten, is she?!

The others agree. Nick gives the drumstick to Nab

Lotaloot I fear you are right, Constable. There *do* seem to be suspicious circumstances at work here! I will organize a search party immediately!

All agree

Nick Just a minute! Just a minute! This is now a police matter! I will take charge!
Lotaloot Very well! What do you propose to do?
Nick I will organize a search party immediately!
Lotaloot (*outraged*) Oh!

Mr X, now playing the Parson, appears at the windows L. *Note: the audience may respond to him with boos and hisses. If so, this should be ignored*

Mr X (*as Parson*) Ah! Here you all are! Oh, dear me! Is there something amiss?
Nick Dame Dollop, Billy Bumpkin and Katie Cuddlesome have disappeared under mysterious circumstances! We are in the middle of a police investigation!
Mr X But ... er... I have just this very moment been in conversation with them.

All react

Oh, believe me, good friends, there is no cause for concern. They have been called back to their farm on urgent business. They asked me to convey their apologies, and hope it will not spoil the rest of the evening's entertainment.

General relief from everyone, except Nick who moves dejectedly DR

Lotaloot Thank ye, Parson, for clearing up that mystery. All's well that ends well, eh? Now! On with the party!

Music. Lotaloot, Caroline, Dick and the guests move upstage to prepare for the next number

Mr X slides out through the windows

Nab goes down to the sulking Nick

Nab (*holding up the drumstick*) 'Ere, Sherlock! What shall I do with this?
Nick Don't tempt me!

He stomps out R. *Eating the drumstick, Nab follows him*

Music up. The others move forward into the song and dance

Song 11

After the song, the Lights fade to Black-out

SCENE 2

The Underground Cell

Tabs, or a frontcloth showing the grey, slimy walls of a grim subterranean chamber

The Lighting is dark and eerie

Dame Dollop is discovered facing upstage, Billy is facing R, *and Katie faces* L. *All three are calling for help. They have been doing this for a long time without success and are now worn out and hoarse*

All (*calling feebly*) 'Elp! 'Elp! Let us out! We're in 'ere! 'Elp, somebody, 'elp! (*Etc. They all give up and face the front*)
Dame Oh, I give up! I can't shout anymore! Me throat's so hoarse you could put a saddle on it! No-one's gonna 'ear us buried down 'ere! We must be miles underneath the 'ouse! We've shouted till we're blue in the face!
Katie An' that baint all that's turnin' blue! (*She shivers and hugs herself with the cold*) Brr! 'Tis cold as ice down 'ere!
Dame (*shivering*) You're right! Talk about frozen assets!

Shivering, they pace up and down, looking at their awesome surroundings

Billy Oh, dung flies! There's *got* to be some way out of 'ere!

Katie So you keep sayin'! But *'ow*?! We be surrounded by solid stone walls! We've got about as much chance of gettin' out as you've got bein' picked fer *Mastermind*!

Billy (*insistent*) But, that Mr X brought us *in*, so there mus' be a way *out*!

Dame Oh, don't you dare mention that nasty so-an-so again! Oo! What a dirty, two-faced double crosser!

Katie Jus' fancy! Pretendin' to be a parson, an' all the time 'e was plannin' to rob 'is Lordship's 'ouse!

Billy An' 'e *will*, if we don't stop 'im!

Dame And how are we goin' to do that when we're stuck 'ere in the Crystal Maze!

Billy Oi 'ave a cunnin' plan!

Dame Oh yes! (*To the audience*) This ought to be good, folks! (*To him*) Don't tell me—we all shout "Open Sesame", slide down the magic beanstalk and turn into pumpkins at midnight!

Billy (*genuinely impressed*) Cor! Thas a good plan too, missus! Reckon it'll work?

Dame (*cuffing him*) You great big wally! Go on, what's your cunnin' plan?

Billy When ole nasty comes back...

Dame Yes?

Billy We jump 'im!

Dame Oh, very clever.

Billy (*proudly*) Ar!

Dame But you're forgettin' something!

Billy Wot?

Dame Something about this long, with a trigger at one end an' a dirty great bullet at the other! (*She starts cuffing him*) You dozy, soppy twit!

The muffled sound of approaching footsteps is heard from off R

Katie Shh! Shh! Listen! What's that?!

They listen. The footsteps draw nearer. The three creep to R, and huddle there, listening

Dame It's ... it's footsteps...! Behind that wall!

Billy Per'aps 'tis a rescue party!

All three shout "'Elp! 'Elp! We're in here! This way! 'Elp!", etc etc. The footsteps stop. A loud grinding sound is heard from off R, as an unseen section of the wall slides back

Look…! The wall be slidin' open!
Katie (*overjoyed*) They've found us!
Dame Hurray!

Holding hands, they skip to C, and dance with joy. The grinding sound stops with a thud

Mr X strides on from R, brandishing his pistol. He is still wearing clerical attire, minus the hat and wig. He takes in the oblivious dancers, then gives his evil laugh

Dame Oh no!
Mr X Turn around!

Quaking with fear, they turn to face L. Mr X keeping the pistol trained on them, finds a "special spot" on the ground R. He stamps his foot there three times. The grinding sound and thud are heard off R

Turn around!
Dame Again! 'E should get a job on the *Magic Roundabout*!

They turn to face Mr X

Mr X (*sneering*) I trust you are quite comfortable here? Is everything to your satisfaction?
Dame (*sarcastic*) Oh, super duper! The (*local "posh" hotel*) couldn't do better!
Mr X I'm so glad. I really want you to enjoy your last few hours.

The others react

Billy (*stammering*) W—wot d'you mean … *last* few 'ours?!
Mr X Oh, come! Even you can't be that dimwitted. It's quite simple. After I have carried out the robbery I intend to kill all three of you! Ha ha ha!
Dame (*laughing with him*) Ha ha ha! (*To the other two*) D'you know, for a minute I thought he said 'e was gonna kill us!

Billy ⎫
Katie ⎬ (*together*) 'E did!
Mr X I am!

Dame Dollop wails and sags between Billy and Katie

Billy B—but why?
Mr X You have discovered my true identity! You have beheld the face
   of Mr X! You have exposed my alias!
Dame We never touched it!
Mr X So! You must be disposed of!

The others cower in mute terror

   And now—turn around!

Trembling, they turn to face L. *He finds the "special spot" and stamps*
three times. The grinding sound and thud are heard off R

   (*Moving to the exit* R) I am going now, but I shall return shortly to— (*in*
   the Parson voice) join you in your prayers and give you the last rites!
   (*He laughs evilly*) Ha ha ha!

   Mr X exits R

The grinding sound and thud are heard off R

Dame (*wailing*) Ooo! I'm too young an' beautiful to die!
Billy (*wailing as well*) So be oi!
Katie (*rounding on Billy*) If you were a real man you'd save us!
Dame If 'e was a *real* man at least we could die 'appy!
Billy Shh! Oi've bin thinkin'!
Dame Oh, this is no time to take up a new hobby!
Billy When Mr X kept tellin' us to turn around, 'e done somethin',
   remember?
Katie Ar! It sounded like 'e were stampin' his foot.
Dame Yes! Then there was a funny noise from over there! (*He points* R)
Billy It were the wall slidin' open! Thas 'ow 'e got it to work—by
   stampin' 'is foot!

Dame Well, what are we waitin' for! Let's get stampin'!

Like things demented, they go all around the stage stamping their feet. Needless to say, they never go anywhere near the "special spot" R. Comic business with Billy stamping on the Dame's toe. Eventually, they get worn out and disheartened

Oh, this is a waste of time! Nothin's 'appenin'! All we've got is a flatter floor, an' bigger bunions! We'll never find the right spot!
Billy Oh yes, we will! (*He indicates the audience*) All our chums out there knows where it is! (*To the audience*) Don't you, folks?

"Yes!" from the audience

Dame Do ya?

"Yes!" from the audience

Katie Will you tell us where to find it?

"Yes!" from the audience

Billy Right then kids! Where be it? Over 'ere?

They move to far L. Comic routine with the audience shouting instructions, while the three on stage keep going in the wrong direction. Finally, they get it right and form a tight group on the "special spot" R

All (*to the audience, pointing to the ground at their feet*) Is it 'ere?

"Yes!" from the audience

Billy (*excited*) Let oi do it! Let oi do it!
Dame Oh, go on, then! An' give it some wellie! (*She points to the ground with her toe*) Right 'ere!

Billy stamps his foot—right on her toe! She yells and hops about. Billy is about to stamp again

Billy (*to the audience*) 'Ow many times do oi 'ave to stamp?

"Three!" from the audience

 (*Gormless*) Er... Thas one an' ... an' er...
Dame (*to the audience*) Oh, 'e's 'opeless at countin'! We'll 'ave to 'elp
 'im kids! Ready!

*Billy stamps his foot with the audience counting "One, Two, Three" for
him. They listen and look to* R. *Nothing*

 Let all three of us try!

Together they stamp their feet, listen and look to R. *Still nothing*

 Not a sausage!
Katie (*desperately*) Wot be us gonna do?!
Dame Well, there's only one thing we *can* do! We'll have to ask our mates
 out there to lend a hand—or in this case—a foot! (*To the audience*)
 You'll 'elp us, folks, won't you? You'd better, or we'll never get into
 the next scene! Now, we want you all to stamp your feet, as loud as you
 can, three times! An' watch out for Gran's corns! Are you ready? Go!

*They get the audience to stamp their feet with them. They listen and look.
Again nothing*

 Let's try again! Louder this time! Ready—steady—*Go*!

They all stamp. The grinding sound is heard off R

Billy 'Tis workin'!
Katie Look! The wall's slidin' open!
All (*to the audience*) Thanks, folks!

*The grinding sound ends with a thud. Led by Billy, they creep right up to
the* R *exit, and peer off into the gloom*

Katie Wot can you see?
Billy Not much... 'Tis all dark an' creepy... There be a sort o' passage-
 way... (*He bends over to peer closer*) Oi wonder where it leads.
Dame Now's yer chance to find out!

She jabs his bottom, sending him flying off R

(*To Katie*) You next! Age before beauty!

She shoves Katie off R

(*To the audience*) See you later—(*gulp*)—I 'ope!

With big exaggerated steps, she creeps off R, *as the Lights fade to Black-out*

SCENE 3

The Garden of Lotaloot Hall

Part of the ivy clad house is seen R *with open french windows leading on to a terrace and steps. Across the back runs a low wall surmounted with ornate urns.* L *is a high wall with an alcove containing a stone seat. The back wall of the alcove slides back to reveal a secret passage. The backcloth shows distant parkland. The wings represent trees and sculptured hedges. There are exits* DR, L *and* UL. *Bright moonlight and strong lighting from the windows illuminate the scene*

All the guests are discovered grouped about watching the dancers or children as they perform a merry dance, accompanied by singing. On the terrace stand Lotaloot and Mr X. Mr X is now back in full clerical attire and playing the Parson. Nick and Nab are sitting on the alcove seat, DL

Song 12

After the number, all the spectators clap and cheer

Lotaloot Bravo! And now, my friends, I will ask you all to proceed to the far side of the gardens, where the firework display will shortly take place! (*He calls to Nick and Nab*) Hey! You two!

They jump up, snap to attention and salute

Make yourselves useful, and show my guests the way!

Nick and Nab bend their knees and salute again. They move up to the guests and usher them UL, *as if they were doing traffic control duty*

Nick ⎫
Nab ⎭ *(together)* This way! This way for the grand firework display! Move along there! This way! *(Etc.)*

They exit with the guests UL

Lotaloot looks about

Lotaloot *(calling; irritably)* Caroline! Caroline! Egad, where is that gal?! *(He hobbles down the steps)*

The Parson assists him

Really, Parson, 'tis too bad of her! I lay on this highly expensive party for her benefit, and this is how she repays me! I'll wager she's off somewhere with that farm boy!

Parson Ah! The ingratitude of youth! You have indeed lavished every luxury on her, my Lord. This splendid house to live in, containing so many wonderful treasures.

Lotaloot *(boastfully)* Ha! My dear Parson, the things you see on display are mere bagatelles! The *prize* possession is my collection of jewels!

Parson Indeed?

Lotaloot Aye! They are worth—— *(He whispers in Mr X's ear)*

Parson *(acting suitably shocked and overwhelmed)* Oh, merciful heavens! I trust you keep them in a very safe place.

Lotaloot To be sure! They are so cunningly concealed that a thousand Dick Turpins would never find 'em!

Parson Really? And where is that, pray?

Lotaloot *(hesitantly)* Well ... er...

Parson Oh, come, my Lord. I am a man of the cloth. You can trust me. Your secret will be quite safe, I assure you.

Lotaloot Yes, why not! *(He looks about, then confides)* In my bedchamber there is a certain chair. It has a secret compartment in the seat, and the jewels are concealed there! Dashed clever, what?

Parson Oh, indeed, my Lord! Most ingenious!

Lotaloot Now, we must not keep the guests waitin' any longer. Come, Parson.

Lotaloot hobbles out UL

Parson (*making as if to follow*) Coming, my Lord. (*He makes sure Lotaloot is out of sight, then turns to the audience; as Mr X*) Ha ha ha! So! I now know where the jewels are hidden! Soon they will be mine! All mine! Ha ha ha!

Parson/Mr X hurries out, DR

Caroline and Dick enter through the windows and come down the steps

Caroline Oh dear! Where is everyone?
Dick Oi reckon they be all gone to watch the firework display.
Caroline Oh yes! It must be time. I had completely forgotten about it. We had better hurry and join the others or Father will be angry. He is already vexed that I've spent so much time with you as it is.
Dick (*moving closer*) Does that worry you?
Caroline Of course not. I—I have enjoyed your company.
Dick (*taking her hands*) Not 'alf as much as oi've enjoyed yours.

They gaze adoringly at each other. The spell is broken by the sound of fireworks being ignited from off L. *At the same time, the night sky behind them is lit up with cascades of colour*

Caroline The fireworks have started! (*She breaks from him and moves to* UL) We must join the others!
Dick (*rushing to her, his accent gone*) Wait...! Caroline...!
Caroline Yes, Dick?
Dick I ... want to ask you something...
Caroline What?

From this point the firework sound effects start to fade out

Dick I—I... (*He resumes his accent*) 'Ave you enjoyed your party?
Caroline Oh yes! (*She moves closer to him*) It's been the most wonderful birthday party I've ever had.
Dick Why be that?
Caroline I think you already know the answer to that question.

Song 13

A romantic duet. It might be nice to dim out the stage lighting and make special use of the firework effects on the backcloth. Perhaps even have the dancers or children enter with lit sparklers, and perform a display behind the two lovers

After the duet, the Lighting reverts back to as it was before the number

The dancers/children, if used, exit quickly UL

The firework lighting and sound effects continue until the end of the scene. The sound effects should not be obtrusive

Dick *(embracing her, his accent forgotten)* Do you really love me, Caroline...? *(He hastily resumes his accent)* Oi, a poor, common muckspreader?
Caroline *(gazing up at him)* I do! I do, with all my heart.
Dick *(accent gone again)* What if... What if I were... Someone else?
Caroline What do you mean?
Dick What if... Oh, darling, I must tell you! *(He takes a deep breath)* I am——

But the sudden entrance of Nick and Nab from UL *prevent him from saying any more. Nick strides on, looking very glum and serious*

The lovers part

(Resuming his accent) Cor! You don't look very 'appy, constable! Wot's the matter? Did someone tie a banger to yer truncheon?

Nab roars with laughter at this. Nick gives him an icy glare and the laughter dies

Nick I'm still not satisfied about Dame Dollop and the others.
Caroline But you heard what Parson Goodfellow said. They were called back to the farm on urgent business.
Nick Yes, miss! But what *sort* of urgent business? Per'aps there's been a break-in! *(Drawing himself up)* I feel it my duty to go to the farm and investigate the matter immediately.
Nab *(protesting)* But they 'aven't finished with the fireworks yet!

Nick (*sternly*) Constable Nab! This is no time to be thinkin' of lettin' off your squib! (*To Dick*) As you work at the farm, I'll be askin' you to assist us. I 'ereby make you a special constable!

Dick salutes and does knee bending routine

Nab (*to the audience, with a wink*) Very nice!

The three of them do the "getting into car" routine and "drive" out DL, *making the siren noise. Dick, "sitting in the back", waves to Caroline as they go out. Laughing, she follows them to the exit, and waves them off*

Lotaloot stumps on from UL, *making for the house. He spots Caroline*

Lotaloot Caroline!
Caroline (*turning and moving up to him*) Oh, hullo, Father.
Lotaloot Zounds, daughter! I am most displeased! I will have words with you in the morning! In the meantime—good night to ye! (*He goes up the steps*)
Caroline (*taking his arm*) Oh, Father dear, I'm sorry if I've displeased you. It's been a marvellous birthday party. Far more wonderful than you can ever imagine! I'm very grateful, believe me. Thank you. (*She kisses him on the cheek*) Please don't be angry with me.
Lotaloot (*softening*) Well—er—we'll say no more about it. (*He pats her hand*) Good night, my dear, and… Happy Birthday. (*He kisses her forehead, then tries to regain his disapproval*) And now, by gad, perhaps you'll spend what's left of the party with yer guests!
Caroline (*laughing*) I will, Father, I promise. Good night and sleep well.

Lotaloot hobbles off into the house

Caroline watches him go, then descends the steps. The "special" low whistle is heard off DR. *Caroline stops and listens. The whistle is repeated. She quickly moves* DL, *and hides in the shadows of the alcove*

Mr X creeps stealthily on from DR. *He now wears the cloak and mask etc. He gives the whistle*

Slowly, the heads of Smash and Grab appear over the wall at the back. They repeat the whistle

Mr X sees them and gestures. They scramble over the wall and join him down stage

Grab Is it time, Mr X?

Smash (*with ghoulish glee*) Do we nick the jewels now, Mr X?!

Mr X Yes, my putrid pair! The time is right! The jewels will soon be in our clutches!

Smash 'Ave you found out where 'e keeps 'em?

Mr X I have! They are concealed in his chamber!

Smash
Grab } (*together; revolted*) Ugh!

Mr X His *bed*chamber!

Smash
Grab } (*together; relieved*) Ah!

Grab Is the 'ouse empty?

Mr X It is! They are all on the far side of the garden, watching the fireworks. Come! Let us be about the deed!

Smash Are you sure there's no-one left inside?

Mr X If there is, he's a dead man! No-one stands in the way of Mr X! Anyone foolish enough to come between me and those jewels gets his throat slit!

Caroline (*gasping, audibly*) Oh no! Father!

The three men react. Caroline, realizing that she has been heard, tries to sink further into the shadows

Grab (*scared*) W—wot was that?

Smash (*whispering*) Mr X, I fink there's someone else 'ere!

Mr X (*snarling at audience*) *Is* there someone else here?!

"No!" from the audience

Oh yes, there is! (*Routine with the audience, then Mr X calls a halt to it*) Enough! (*To the others*) Take no notice of these mindless morons! If there is someone here, we'll soon flush 'em out! Get searching!

Fanning out, they move to the back and search about. Thinking it is now safe, Caroline emerges from hiding

Caroline (*to the audience*) Have they gone?

The villains hear her, spin around and creep silently up behind her. The audience will be shouting "No! They're behind you!", "Look behind you", etc. Eventually, Caroline sees them and tries to run away, but Smash and Grab seize her. Mr X quickly ties a gag over her mouth. She struggles in vain

Grab Wot we gonna do wiv 'er, Mr X?

Smash She musta 'eard our plans!

Mr X Yes! For that she will suffer the same fate as the other three fools! Quickly! Bring her this way! (*He rushes to the alcove and leaps on to the seat. He manipulates a piece of carving*)

The back wall of the alcove slides away to reveal a dark passage

Take her through!

Smash and Grab bundle the struggling Caroline out through the opening

Mr X gives the audience his evil laugh, shakes his fist, and follows the others

The panel starts to close. Bring up the sound effects of fireworks as the Light fade to Black-out

Scene 4

The Underground Cell

Tabs, or the frontcloth used in Act II, Scene 2

The Lighting is dark and eerie. To open, the stage is empty and silent, then voices are heard off R

Dame (*off; with a yell of pain*) Ahooow! Watch it, you clumsy great clot! That's my foot!

Billy (*off*) Sorry!

Dame (*off*) What ya stopped for anyway? Keep on walkin'!

Billy (*off*) Oi don't reckon we'm goin' the right way.

Katie (*off*) You're goin' the right way to get a thick ear!
Dame (*off*) Oh, stop messin' about, Billy, and get movin'!
Billy (*off*) But, oi don't reckon...
Dame ⎱
Katie ⎰ (*off; together*) Move!

Billy is shoved on from R, and lands on the floor. He picks himself up and looks around

Dame (*off; calling*) Find anythin'?!
Billy (*calling back*) Ar! But you baint gonna like it!

Dame Dollop and Katie enter from R. They both look bedraggled and dusty

Welcome 'ome!

They look about and groan

Dame Oh no! It's the (*local establishment*) again! We're right back where we started from!
Katie (*rounding on him*) This be all your fault, Billy Bumpkin! You were supposed to be gettin' us out of 'ere!
Dame Yes! A fine Indiana Jones you turned out to be!

They start hitting him

Billy (*warding them off*) Ahoow! Stop it! T'aint my fault! All they passages look the same in the dark!
Dame Some party this turned out to be! I've been chucked up a chimney, dragged through drains, caught by the catacombs, and now I'm waitin' to be vandalized by a villainous vicar!
Katie (*getting in a panic*) Oh, wot be us gonna do! 'E'll be comin' back to kill us! Ooo!
Dame Now, Katie! Don't get historical!
Katie If only Dick Turpin were 'ere! 'E'd save us! Oh, Dick! My 'ero! Where are you?!
Dame Tucked up in bed with Jackie Collins if 'e's got any sense!
Katie (*wailing*) Ooo! Oi be scared!
Billy (*going to put his arm around her*) Oh, Katie...

Katie (*flaring at him*) Not *that* scared! (*She clings to the Dame and wails*) Waaah!

Dame Oh no! She's turned the taps on again! (*She grimaces*) I've 'ad one bath this year already! Do somethin', Billy!

Billy Oi know! Oi'll do wot oi always do when *oi* gets scared!

Dame (*horrified*) No, please! Not in this confined space!

Billy Oi'll whistle!

Song 14

Billy sings and whistles, then encourages Katie and the Dame to join him. They try, but keep bursting into tears. He calls on the audience to help him out. By the end, Katie and the Dame are in a worse state than when they started

Dame (*to the audience, tearfully*) Thanks very much! That's cheered me up no end!

Katie Wot be us gonna do?!

Billy We'll 'ave to try our luck in the passages again! Come on!

They all move to the exit R, but pull up short

Dame Shh! Listen!

The sound of approaching footsteps is heard from off R

Billy Too late! 'E's comin' back!

Katie (*wailing*) Ooow!

Dame I wish I'd stayed 'ome!

They cower away to far L, and cling to each other in terror

Mr X strides on from R. He is still wearing the cloak and mask, and brandishes his pistol. He gives his evil laugh

Dame (*to the audience, full of gloom*) I wish I 'ad some of what 'e's on!

Mr X So! I see you managed to discover how to operate the secret panel! Very clever! (*He moves to them, sneering*) You didn't get very far, did you?!

Billy (*stammering*) 'Ave you c—come to k—kill us?

Mr X Not yet! Have patience. I have brought a little friend to join you. (*He calls off* R) Bring her in!

Smash and Grab enter from R, *dragging the still gagged Caroline*

The others react

Billy ⎫
Katie ⎬ (*together*) Miss Caroline!
Dame ⎭

Mr X pushes Caroline over to them. She pulls off the gag

Caroline (*yelling*) Help! Somebody! Help!
Mr X Ha ha! Call away! No-one will hear you down here! Ha ha ha ha ha ha ha!
Smash (*tapping Mr X on the shoulder and interrupting his laughter*) I 'ates to spoil yer fun, Mr X, but I reckons we ought to be gettin' a move on, like.
Grab Yus! Them fireworks'll be over soon, an' we aint lifted the jewels yet.
Mr X (*snarling at them*) I know! Don't try to tell me how *to do my job*!
Grab (*aside to Smash, very offended*) Huh! You jus' can't 'elp *some* people, can ya!
Mr X (*casually to the Dame, etc*) I have come to the decision not to shoot you after all.

They react with joy

No, I am going to let you die from starvation instead!

They react with horror

Once I have destroyed the mechanism that operates the secret panel you will be entombed in here forever! No way in! No way out! Ha ha ha! (*To the cronies*) Come! Let us get to those jewels!

The villains rush out R

The others are too horrified to move. The grinding sound is heard from off R. *This galvanizes them into action*

Billy Quick! Stop 'em closin' the panel!

Billy and Dame Dollop rush off R

Katie and Caroline remain at the entrance, looking off. Billy and the Dame are heard struggling to hold back the closing panel. The grinding sound continues

Dame (*off*) Uggghr…! 'Old it…! Don't let it shut…!
Billy (*off*) Oi… Oi… Can't…! Ugghr…!
Dame (*off*) Use somethin' to … wedge it … open…! Ahhh! Not my head…! Ahoooow! An' not *those* either…!
Billy (*off*) Look out!

A loud thud is heard as the panel closes up. It is quickly followed by the sound of hammering and splintering as the mechanism is smashed

Billy and Dame Dollop rush back on and go straight to the "special" spot, DR. *They stamp their feet three times, getting the audience to participate. They listen. Nothing*

Dame Well, that's it, folks! We've 'ad it! Open up them pearly gates!
Caroline But we *must* get out of here! My father's life is at stake! The one in the mask said he'd kill anyone who stood in his way! My father is alone in the house with the jewels at this very moment!
Dame But *'ow*? We're sealed up tighter than a duck's derrière!

They pause to reflect on their grim situation

Caroline (*struck by a thought*) One moment! I may be able to help! When I was a little girl, an old servant showed me all around these secret passages. I seem to remember being brought in here, and … and I'm sure there were *two* entrances. (*She tries to remember, moves about and examines the cell*)

In a tight, eager group, the others follow closely behind her

It … it was a long time ago, and … and I was very small, but… (*She moves to far* L)

The others follow

But... I *think* it was on *this* side! The servant did something, and ... yes!
The wall slid open! Oh, I wish I could remember what it was he did!
Billy Did 'e stamp 'is foot?
Caroline Yes! That's it! I remember now! He *did* stamp his foot!
Billy Three times?
Caroline Yes! Three times! Right about... (*She finds and points to a
"special spot"* DL) Here! Oh, how clever you are, Billy!
Billy (*very proudly*) Oh, ar!
Dame Oh, don't keep tellin' 'im 'e's got a brain, or it'll go to is 'ead! Come
on then, it's stampin' time again!

They get near the "special spot"

(*To the audience*) Now, you know what to do, folks! Three times, as
loud as you can! Right? Ready—steady—*go*!

*Business as they get the audience to stamp with them, then listen. The
grinding sound and thud are heard from off* L. *They all rush to the exit* L
and look off

All (*cheering and giving the audience the thumbs up sign*) Hurray!
Caroline (*nearest to the exit*) I'd better lead the way. I think I can
remember how to get us back into the house. Now, we must stay close
together, so we'd better hold hands. (*She takes Billy's left hand*)

*He enjoys this, and goes all soppy. Katie is not happy with this arrange-
ment! Comic business as she changes place with Billy and pushes him to
the end of the line where he holds the Dame's hand*

Caroline leads them off L, *in a single file. Billy stops to wave goodbye
to the audience, and is hauled out by the Dame as the Lights fade to
Black-out*

SCENE 5

Lord Lotaloot's Bedroom

*The back wall and wings are painted to represent dark oak panelling. Set
in the back wall are two secret panels, one* RC *and one* LC. *These open like
ordinary doors, and are cleverly constructed and painted to look like well*

filled bookcases. A dark passageway runs the full length of the area behind the doors. Between the panels is a carved wooden chair. Its seat lifts up to reveal a secret compartment. Exits R *and* L

To open, the room is empty. The Lighting is dim and slightly spooky

Slowly, the RC *panel opens and Mr X's head appears. He looks about the room, then enters, signalling to Smash and Grab, who creep on behind him*

Grab Is this where 'e keeps the jewels?
Mr X Yes! This is the place. Now we must find that chair with the secret compartment. Get searching!

They look about down stage. A loud yawn is heard from off L

The three react, then dash out RC, *closing the panel behind them*

Lord Lotaloot enters from L. *He is wearing a long nightshirt and tasselled nightcap. His foot is still bandaged. He yawns and stretches*

Lotaloot Egad! That party has quite tired me out. I shall sleep well tonight, foot or no foot! Now, there was something I had to do before getting into bed… What was it? (*To someone in the audience*) No, no! I've already done *that*… Ah, yes! I have to inspect my collection of lovely jewels! (*He goes up to the chair, lifts the seat, and extracts a velvet draw-string bag*)

The UC *panel opens and Mr X peers out*

Moving down stage, Lotaloot opens the bag and runs his fingers lovingly through the sparkling jewels. Mr X creeps out

Smash and Grab follow, leaving the panel open

All three brandish daggers. They fan out, and creep up behind Lotaloot. The audience will be shouting warnings to him

What is it? What are you shouting about? What's the matter? Behind me?! Is there someone behind me?! Are they after my jewels? Well, by thunder, they won't get 'em!

Clutching the bag, he dashes R, *but finds Smash there, brandishing his knife. Going* L, *he comes up against Grab. He tries up stage, but encounters Mr X. They close in on him, then lean backwards with their daggers raised to strike. Just in time, Lotaloot drops to his knees and the villains topple into each other above him*

Lotaloot scuttles away on his knees, gets up and runs out L

Mr X (*disentangling himself from the other two*) After him! Get those jewels!

He dashes out L, *followed by Smash and Grab*

The RC *panel opens, and Caroline enters, followed by Katie, Billy and the Dame. They are still holding hands. They leave the panel open*

Dame (*blinking and looking around*) Where are we? Is it (*local pub/ club*)?
Caroline This is my father's bedroom.
Dame Ooo! Me in a man's bedroom. Me, a susceptible rinster! What will the neighbours think!
Billy That you be lost!

Lotaloot runs on from L, *still clutching the jewel bag. He is being chased by Smash and Grab*

Lotaloot Help! Robbery! They're after my jewels...! Help...!

They run out through the RC *panel*

Caroline (*running out after them*) Father...! Father...!

Caroline exits

Billy (*running out after her*) Miss Caroline...! Come back...!

Billy exits

Katie (*running out after him*) Billy...! Wait fer oi...!

Katie exits

Dame Dollop watches them go, then turns to the audience

Dame Well! I never get this much action in *my* bedroom!

Mr X runs on from L

(*Speaking to him absently*) Do you? (*She does a double take*) Oh no! It's the masked marauder again!
Mr X (*snarling at her and brandishing his dagger*) Ahgggr!
Dame (*yelling*) Ahhhhh!

Mr X chases her out RC

There follows a rapid chase sequence, accompanied by suitable "hurry" music. The actions described in the following notes are only suggestions. Individual directors may have their own ideas or find it necessary to adapt to suit their facilities

(1) Lotaloot, still with the bag, runs on from LC, *being chased by Smash and Grab, and out* RC

(2) Caroline, Billy and Katie run on from LC *and out* RC

(3) Dame Dollop runs on from LC, *being chased by Mr X, and out* RC

(4) Smash and Grab, now with the bag, run on from LC, *being chased by Lotaloot and Caroline and out* RC

(5) Mr X runs on from LC, *being chased by the Dame. Halfway across, they realize their mistake, turn, and Mr X chases Dame Dollop out* LC

(6) Katie runs on from RC, *being chased by Billy, and out* LC

(7) Smash and Grab, still with the bag, run on from RC, *being chased by Lotaloot and Caroline, and out* LC

(8) Billy runs on from LC. *At the same time, Katie runs on from* RC. *They*

meet in the middle and Katie slaps Billy's face. He falls flat on the floor and she runs out LC

(9) Caroline and Lotaloot, now with the bag, run on from RC, *being chased by Smash and Grab. They all jump over Billy and out* LC

(10) Dame Dollop runs on from RC, *being chased by Mr X. They jump over Billy and out* LC

(11) Billy staggers to his feet, dazed. Katie runs on from RC. *She slaps Billy again and he falls to the floor. She runs out* LC

(12) Caroline and Lotaloot, still with the bag, run on from RC, *being chased by Smash and Grab. They jump over Billy and out* LC

(13) Dame Dollop and Mr X run on from RC, *being chased by the Thing (this can be a ghost, a monster or a skeleton!) They all jump over Billy and out* LC

(14) Billy staggers to his feet, dazed. Smash and Grab, now with the bag, run on from RC, *being chased by Lotaloot, Caroline and Katie. On the way, they bump into Billy knocking him to the floor. They run out* LC

(15) Billy sits up, very dazed. The Thing runs on from RC. *It stops and helps Billy to his feet. It even dusts him off! Billy shakes the Thing's hand, then does a huge double take. He screams and runs out* LC. *The Thing turns to the audience and shrugs*

(16) Dame Dollop runs on from RC, *being chased by Mr X. She and the Thing come face to face. It screams and runs out* LC. *Mr X chases Dame Dollop out* LC

(17) Billy runs on from RC, *followed by Katie, Smash and Grab, still with the bag, Caroline and Lotaloot. They are being chased out* LC *by the Thing*

(18) Dame Dollop runs on from RC, *being chased by Mr X, and out* LC. *They re-appear at* RC, *and the Dame runs out* LC. *Mr X casually sits on the chair. Dame Dollop continues to run in and out of the panels several more times, unaware that she is not being chased. Finally, bow legged and completely exhausted, she signals to the conductor/pianist to cut the music and it*

stops. Gasping for breath, she staggers up to the chair and, without realizing it, sits on Mr X's lap. She gets her breath back

(*To the audience*) Phew! I think I've given 'im the slip.
Mr X Oh no, you haven't!

Yelling, she leaps up and runs out LC, *with Mr X chasing her*

A slight pause

Billy and Katie creep on from RC. *They have the jewel bag, and move* DR, *examining it*

Note: the following sequence should be played in a straight line across the stage with all the characters entering from L

Smash runs on and snatches the bag from Katie. Caroline runs on and snatches it from him. Grab runs on and snatches it from her. Dame Dollop runs on and snatches it from him. She holds it up as the victor. Mr X runs on, snatches it from her, and moves DL. *He carries his pistol. Smash and Grab move down* R. *The others huddle together* C

(*Gloating over the bag*) Ha ha ha! At last! The jewels are mine! All mine! Ha ha ha!
Dame (*boldly marching up to him*) You know what you are, don't ya?!
Mr X (*sticking the pistol under her nose*) What?!
Dame (*gulping*) Y—you're a very n—naughty boy! (*She retreats to the others*)
Mr X Bah! I've had enough of you meddlesome fools! The time has come to silence you once and for all! (*He raises the pistol and takes aim at the cringing group*)
Lotaloot (*off* R; *calling*) Help...! Robbery...! Help!

This distracts Mr X and his cronies

The others seize the opportunity and make their escape through the panels at the back. Billy and Katie, RC. *Caroline and Dame Dollop,* LC

Smash and Grab make to give chase

Mr X Let them go! By the time they've found their way out of those passages, we'll be miles away! (*He points off* L) Quick! Out through that window and make your getaway! We'll meet up at the hide-out and divide the jewels! Go!

Smash and Grab dash out L

(*To the audience*) Ha ha ha! There will be no sharing out of these beauties! (*He hugs the jewel bag*) They are all mine! Those two fools will never see the jewels or Mr X ever again! Ha ha ha!

Laughing his evil laugh, Mr X dashes out LC

Lotaloot runs on from R *and straight out* L

Lotaloot (*running across*) Help...! Thieves...! I've been robbed...! Help!

Lotaloot exits L

The Thing runs on from R. *It becomes aware it is alone and shrugs to the audience. It goes up to the chair, lifts the seat and takes out a (local) newspaper. Sitting on the chair, it opens the paper and proceeds to read, as the Lights fade to Black-out*

SCENE 6

A Country Lane, earlier

Tabs, or a frontcloth. Exits DR *and* L

Moonlight

Nick and Dick enter from L. *They get to* C, *and stop*

Nick (*pointing to off* R) Dame Dollop's farm is just around that next bend. We'd better approach it with caution. If there *is* a break-in in progress, we don't want to scare 'em off before we get a chance to nick 'em! Now,

Constable Nab, I want you to... (*He looks around*) Oh, where *is* he...?! (*He goes to* L, *and calls off*) Constable Nab!

Nab (*popping out from* L) Wos up?

Nick (*exasperated*) Wos up?! I'll give you *wos up*, you incompetent copper, you! Don't you realize we're responding to an A. P. B. call! What were you doin?!

Nab (*with a wink*) Respondin' to another type of call! (*He giggles*)

Daisy (*off* R) Moooo!

The others react. Nab is terrified and clings to Nick, who is also scared but tries not to show it

Nab Waaaah! W—what was that?!

Nick I—It's nothing...! Control yerself...! I—It's j—just a b—bird!

Daisy (*off* R; *louder*) Moooo!

Nab A bird?! I'd 'ate to see what kind of bird makes a noise like that!

Daisy (*off* R; *even louder*) Mooooooo!

Nick and Nab shiver and shake

Dick (*looking* R) 'Tis comin' from over there. Didn't we ought to go an' investigate?

Nick G—good idea, *special* constable Appleseed! Off you go, lad. Let it be your first assignment!

Dick Righto!

Dick bends his knees, salutes and exits R

Nervously, Nick and Nab move to far L, *where they talk in hushed tones*

Nab Didn't we ought to go to his assistance?

Nick No. He'll radio if 'e needs backup.

Nab (*nodding in agreement*) Yeah! 'Ere! Radios ain't been invented yet!

Nick Good.

Dick re-appears R

Dick (*calling to them*) Oy!

Nick
Nab } (*together, jumping with fright*) Whaaaah!

Dick No need to panic, chaps. Oi've found the cause of the disturbance.

He reaches off R *and leads on Daisy*

T'was only Daisy! Dame Dollop's pet cow.

Nab (*to Nick*) Ha! Some bird! I'd 'ate to be underneath when *that* was flyin' over!

Dick leads Daisy to C, *where they gather around her*

Dick What be you doin' out on yer own at this time o'night, Daisy? What's 'appened at the farm?

Nick Leave this to me. I'll do the questionin'! Tell me, Miss Cow, how many of them are there?

Daisy (*"What?"*) Moo?

Nick The burglars! Is it Dick Turpin?

Daisy (*to Dick; "What's he talking about?"*) Moo! Moo! Moo! Moo?

Dick (*to Nick*) Let oi try. (*To Daisy*) Why did Dame Dollop an' the others get called away from the party?

Daisy (*shrugging; "How should I know"*) Moo! Moo! Moo!

Dick (*with mounting suspicion*) Are they at the farm now?

Daisy (*shaking her head*) Moo!

Dick Did they come back at all?

Daisy (*shaking her head*) Moo!

The others react

Nick You know what this means, don't you?

Nab Yes! We must be crackers, standin' 'ere talkin' to a *cow*.

Nick No! It means they never *left* Lotaloot Hall! There's some dirty work goin' on up there, and *I'm* gonna get to the bottom of it! (*To emphasize the point, he slaps Daisy on the rump*)

She reacts. Nick looks at his hand and does a grimace

Nab (*smirking*) Looks like you already 'ave!

Nick Quick! Back to Lotaloot Hall at once!

Dick You two go ahead! Oi'll follow as soon as oi've made sure everythin' be safe on the farm!

Nick and Nab run out L, making the siren noise. Daisy gallops out after them, mooing loudly

(*To the audience, as himself*) Good friends, 'tis my belief that the villain who has so blackened my name is responsible for tonight's skullduggery! I also fear that my beloved Caroline is in some deadly peril! I go now to rescue her and clear my good name! The time has come to throw off this disguise and face the challenge as my true self—bold Dick Turpin!

Note: if more time is required for the scene change, a song may be added here, but only if absolutely necessary

Dick gives the audience a swashbuckling salute and runs out R, as the Lights fade to Black-out

SCENE 7

The Garden of Lotaloot Hall

The same setting as Act II, Scene 3, with the same Lighting minus the firework effects

To open, the stage is empty. Lord Lotaloot is heard calling loudly and desperately from inside the house

Lotaloot (*off* R) Help...! Thieves...! Robbers...! Help...! Help...!

Smash and Grab run on from DR. They pause to make sure the coast is clear, then run out DL

The back wall of the alcove slides open, and Mr X creeps cautiously out. He is now dressed as the Parson and clutches the jewel bag. Leaving the panel open, he looks about, then moves to C

Mr X (*gloating over the bag and giving the audience his evil, sneering laugh*) Ha ha ha! Hee hee!
Guests (*off* UL; *overlapping*) Who was that shouting?! I say, what's going on?! It came from the house! What's happening?! Is it a fire?! This way! (*Etc, etc*)

Mr X hastily puts the bag in his coat pocket and assumes the stance and manner of Parson Goodfellow

The guests rush on from UL

Man Parson Goodfellow! What's happening?
Woman We heard cries for help!
Parson So did I! Oh, dear! I hope there hasn't been a calamity!
Man (*pointing to the house*) Look!

Lotaloot, in a state of near collapse, staggers on through the windows

General reaction. The Parson and a couple of the guests rush over and assist him down the steps

Parson Good heavens! My Lord, what's the matter? Are you ill?
Lotaloot (*gasping*) I—I've been robbed! My jewels! They've stolen my jewels…!
Parson Who?
Lotaloot Three vile villains! They broke in, and… Where are those constables…?! Send for the constables!
Parson Pray compose yourself, my Lord. I will go at once and fetch them.
Lotaloot Make haste! Make haste! Oo! My jewels…! (*He sags into the arms of the guests*)

The guests gather around him

Parson (*aside to the audience*) Now to make my escape!

He hurries to the exit DL, *but pulls up short as Nick enters there, dragging on Smash. Grab is pushed on by Nab*

Nick We just happrehended these two characters, runnin' away from the 'ouse, in what seemed a 'ighly suspicious manner!
Lotaloot It's them! They're the ones! The ones who stole my jewels!

General reaction

Smash We never did!

Nick (*to him*) Shut it, you! (*To Lotaloot*) Are you sayin' you've had property stolen tonight, m'lud?

Lotaloot Yes! My jewel collection! By those two blackguards! Egad! I saw 'em do it with me own eyes!

Nick I knew there was dirty work goin' on! (*To Smash, clamping his hands on his shoulder*) You're nicked, sonny Jim!

Lotaloot Give me back those jewels, you scoundrels!

Smash We ain't got 'em! 'Onest, we ain't, guv'nor!

Grab Naw! It was Mr X! '*E's* got 'em!

Nick Mr X?! Who's Mr X?

Smash Dunno! We only know 'im as Mr X! It was all '*is* idea, guv'nor! (*All innocence*) We didn't know what we was doin'! We was lead atray!

Grab Yus! I plead insanitary!

Lotaloot (*to Nick*) There *was* a third man! He seemed to be the ringleader! He wore a black mask!

Parson A black mask? Dick Turpin! Dick Turpin is this Mr X, and he's stolen your jewels!

Lotaloot Zounds! You're right, Parson!

Dame Dollop suddenly appears in the alcove opening

Dame Oh, no, 'e's not! An' 'e's not a Parson either!

General reaction, as the Dame descends to the stage

She is followed by Caroline, Billy and Katie

Caroline Father! (*She points to Mr X*) That man is an imposter!

General sensation

Lotaloot (*dumbfounded*) W—what…?!

Billy 'E's no more a parson than oi'm Hugh Grant! (*Or any other newsworthy person*)

Parson (*trying to laugh it off*) Is this some merry jest?

Dame An' you can cut the phoney voice! The game's up, buster!

Parson (*appealing to Lotaloot*) My Lord, this is outrageous…!

Caroline We speak the truth, Father. He's a robber in disguise! You must believe us!

Lotaloot (*confused and blustering*) Well, er… I…

Dame Oh, I've 'ad enough of this beatin' about the bush! I'll prove it! (*She lunges forward and whips off the Parson's hat and wig*)

General sensation and uproar. Mr X, realizing the game is up, pulls out a dagger and swings it around in a wide arc. With gasps, everyone backs away from him

Lotaloot Gadzooks! 'Tis true...! Constables...! *Do* something!
Nick (*to Mr X, timidly*) P—put that down... Y—you'll hurt somebody...
Mr X (*snarling and making play with the dagger*) How right you are! Ha ha ha!
Nick G—give yourself up... Y—you can't get away...!
Mr X Oh, can't I?! (*He suddenly grabs Caroline, pulls her towards him, and holds the dagger to her throat*)

Screams and gasps from the others. Using Caroline as a shield, Mr X backs away to the exit DR

I warn you! If anyone tries to stop me or attempts to follow, I will slit her throat!

Dick enters from DR. *He wears his highwayman outfit with cloak and mask etc., and carries a drawn sword*

Dick Hold!
Mr X (*spinning around, still holding Caroline in front of him*) Who the devil...!
Dick I am Dick Turpin! Release that woman, you coward, and fight like a man! (*He strikes a challenging pose with his sword*)
Mr X One step nearer and she dies!

He brings the dagger closer to Caroline's throat. She grabs his hand and bites it. Yelling, he drops the knife. Struggling free, Caroline runs back to Lotaloot and the others

Dick Now 'tis just the two of us! (*To the crowd*) Someone give him a blade!

One of the guests draws his sword, and nervously gives it to Mr X. Dick assumes the stance

On guard!

To suitable music, Dick and Mr X engage in a fencing duel. The others move back to give them plenty of room. The duel should be as elaborate and spectacular as possible. (See Production Notes) During a clinch, Mr X pushes Dick away and draws a pistol. Gasps and exclamations from the onlookers

Mr X Ha ha ha! Prepare to die, Dick Turpin! (*He takes aim at Dick*)

Billy dashes forward and wrenches the pistol from his hand. With it, he scuttles back to the others. The duel continues. Eventually, Dick disarms Mr X who falls to the ground. Dick plants his foot on the fallen villain, and holds his sword aloft in triumph. The music stops

Others (*cheering*) Hurray!

Mr X's sword and dagger are quickly cleared by the guests

Dick (*to Mr X*) And now, my villainous friend, before you are taken to your richly deserved prison cell, I want you to make a confession before this assembly. Are you the one responsible for the recent foul crimes for which I, Dick Turpin, have been unjustly blamed?

No answer. Dick puts the point of his sword to Mr X's throat

Answer!
Mr X Yes!

General sensation

Katie (*ecstatically*) Oi knew it! Oi knew it! (*To the others*) Oi told ee so!
Dick At last! The good name of Dick Turpin has been restored!
Lotaloot (*moving to Dick, a little nervously*) Er ... he stole my jewels...
   Make him give them back...
Dick (*with a bow*) Certainly, my Lord! (*To all*) Witness all of you! This
   shall be my last act as a highwayman! (*To Mr X*) You, there! Stand and
   deliver! (*He steps back and holds out his hand*)

Mr X gets to his feet. He takes the jewel bag from his pocket and morosely gives it to Dick. With a flourish, Dick hands it to Lotaloot

Your jewels, my Lord!

Lotaloot (*clutching the bag, lovingly*) Oh, thank ye! Thank ye! (*To Nick*) Remove these blackguards! Lock 'em in the town jail immediately!

Nick (*marching over*) With pleasure, m'lud! (*He clamps his hand on Mr X's shoulder*) Come on—*your reverence*! (*He leads him over to join Smash and Grab*)

Nab (*with a big grin*) You three are goin' down!

Amid jeers from the others, Nick and Nab take the three villains out DL. *They snarl and shake their fists at the audience as they go*

Lotaloot Master Turpin, you remind me of someone, but I'm dashed if I know who it is!

Dick Perhaps this will help, my Lord! (*He whips off his mask, and speaks with the accent*) Do ee know who oi be now? (*He laughs*)

General sensation

Lotaloot Egad! 'Tis the hand kissin' clodhopper!

Dame Dick Appleseed!

Caroline (*rushing into Dick's arms*) Darling!

More exclamations—most of them from Katie

Lotaloot (*stunned*) Daughter! W—what is the meaning of this ... *this*?!

Caroline Dick and I love each other, Father!

Dick That we do, sir!

Katie Ooo! 'E loves another! My 'ero! My 'ero! (*She starts wailing*) Waaaaahh!

Billy (*going to her*) Oh, Katie...

Katie (*pushing him away*) Oh, leave oi alone, you!

Dick Katie! That's no way to treat a hero.

Katie Huh?!

Dick Billy's a hero now! Didn't he save my life just now when that villain tried to blow my head off? Surely that makes him a *super* hero!

Katie (*mulling this over*) Wull, oi... (*Elated*) Ar! You'm right! Billy! My 'ero! (*She throws her arms around Billy's neck and kisses him*)

He is startled, to say the least! Perhaps the pistol he is still holding can go off with a loud bang? Everyone laughs and cheers

Lotaloot But I protest! Odd's life! I can't allow my only daughter to be in love with a highwayman!

Dick *Ex*-highwayman, my Lord. I henceforth give up my life of crime! I intend to become an honest man and get a job!

Lotaloot But what sort of job can an *ex*-highwayman *do*?!

Dick I understand there's an opening at (*local*) tax office!

Lotaloot (*aside, to the audience*) Most suitable! (*To Dick*) Very well, if it makes my Caroline happy, I give ye both my blessing! (*He shakes hands with Dick*)

Cheers and jubilation. Caroline and Dick embrace, so do Billy and Katie

Dame (*overjoyed*) Ooo! Isn't it dead romantic! There's marriage in the air! (*She looks at Caroline and Dick*) We'll be goin' to a weddin' soon! (*She looks at Katie and Billy*) A *double* weddin', I shouldn't wonder! (*She goes to Lotaloot and gives him a nudge*) Wouldn't it be nice to make it a *triple*! (*She flutters her eyelashes at him*) Know wot I mean? Nudge, nudge! Wink, wink!

Lotaloot (*puzzled*) I don't grasp your meaning Dame Dollop.

Dame Oh, don't worry! *I'll* do the graspin'! (*She moves in very close to him—standing on his bad foot in the process. In a deep, sexy voice*) Ooo, my Lord!

Lotaloot Ooo, my foot! (*He hops about and yelps in agony*)

Dame (*watching him*) Hey! That's a good idea! (*To all*) Let's 'ave a song an' dance to celebrate the 'appy endin'!

The music starts and they all go into a joyful song and dance

Song 15

After the song, a front cloth is lowered or the tabs close

SCENE 8

The Bit Before the Last Bit

Frontcloth or tabs

Billy enters

Billy (*calling to the audience and waving*) 'Ello, folks!

They call back

Eh? Oi didn't 'ear that! Try again! (*He calls louder*) 'Ello, folks!

They call back

Ar! Thas better! Wull, did you enjoy it?

"Yes!" from the audience

Why, wot were you doin'? (*He guffaws*) Ar! It all turned out 'appy ever after! That were a big surprise, weren't it? Now, before we go, Daisy, the cow, wants to say goodbye. She be a bit shy so you'll 'ave to 'elp oi call 'er out. After three, then! One—two—three!

He and the audience call

Daisy! (*He looks towards the wings*) Nope! Oi don't reckon she 'eard that. Try again.

They call

Daisy! (*He goes to one side and looks off*) Nope! And again—*Daisy!*

Daisy pokes her head on from the opposite side

'As she come out, kids? Wull, where is she? (*etc.*)

Daisy trots across and gives him a playful nudge

Now then, old girl, say goodbye to all the nice people.
Daisy (*to the audience*) Moooo!
Billy (*to the audience*) Now you say—Goodbye Daisy!

They do so. Daisy gives them a curtsy

Dame (*off*) Hurray! Whoopee!

The Dame rushes on in great excitement. She wears a comical outfit that can be easily changed for the Finale

Ooo! Billy! Daisy! Oo! You'll never guess what's 'appened! 'Is Lordship! 'E's asked me to marry 'im—and I've accepted! Ooo! (*To the audience*) At last it's 'appened, folks! At last I shall be someone's *awful* wedded wife! An' I'll be a *real* lady then girls! (*Nose in the air*) Lady Lotaloot! Oo! I'm so excited, I feel like singin'!

Billy (*to the audience*) There's a cue fer a song if ever oi 'eard one!

Dame (*to the audience*) Yes! Why don't we *all* sing! Ha ha! You thought you'd got away with it, didn't you?! (*She calls off*) Let's 'ave a decko at the ditty!

A song sheet is lowered or can be brought on by members of the chorus. Dame Dollop, Billy and Daisy have fun getting the audience to sing

Song 16

After the song, the song sheet is removed

They wave goodbye to the audience and run out. Daisy gives the audience a curtsy and trots out after the others, as the Lights fade to Black-out

SCENE 9

The Finale

A special setting or the garden scene can be used with modifications

Bright Lighting

Music

All enter singing for the Finale walk down. The last to enter are Dick and Caroline

Dick The time has come to say Adieu!

Caroline Our fondest wishes go out to you.

Nick Dick Turpin sorted out the mess.
Nab And *still* no sign of his horse—Black Bess!
Katie Billy's the best! 'E's now—*my 'ero*!
Billy Steady girl! That were right in my ear 'ole!
Lotaloot (*to Dame Dollop*) My family jewels shall be yours, egad!
Dame I'll give 'em the best polishin' they've ever 'ad!
Mr X I'll get my revenge! This day you'll rue!
Billy And Daisy says——
Daisy Moo! Moo! Moo! Moo!
Dame You've all been good, not much coughin' or burpin'!
All Goodnight and God Bless—from bold Dick Turpin!

Finale Song 17

CURTAIN

FURNITURE AND PROPERTY LIST

Further dressing may be added at the director's discretion

ACT I

SCENE 1

On stage: Bales of straw
Farming implements
Plastic bucket
Milking stool

Off stage: Feed pail (**Katie**)
Cloak, hat and mask (**Dick**)

Personal: **Nick:** "Wanted" poster, huge magnifying glass, police whistle
Nab: blue flashing light on hat, police whistle
Lotaloot: quizzing glass, snuff box (throughout)
Caroline: drawstring bag. *In it:* purse
Daisy: fake milk bottle, box of Milk Tray
Billy: hat covered in straw

SCENE 2

Off stage: Large shopping bag. *In it:* cake with "file" candle, pliers, stick of dynamite, hacksaw (**Dame**)

Personal: **Dame:** rope ladder around waist

SCENE 3

On stage: **Judge**'s bench. *On it:* gavel, black cap, quill pen, books and papers
Judge's chair
Judicial coat of arms
Benches
Dock rostrum

Off stage: Picnic hampers, camping stools, butterfly nets (**Chorus and Children**)
Hot dog, ice cream and drink trays (**Dancers**)
Long rope, ball and chain, manacles (**Billy**)
Bundle of papers (**Dame**)

Personal: **Nick:** whistle, long scroll
Lotaloot: bandage on foot, walking stick
Dick: 2 pistols, money bag
Judge: wig

SCENE 4

Personal: **Lotaloot:** foot bandage and stick

SCENE 5

Off stage: Round sieve with thin paper top (**Katie**)
Table and chairs, various props for optional slapstick routine (**Nick** and **Nab**)

ACT II

SCENE 1

On stage: Long, gilt framed mirrors
Portraits
Large fireplace (secret passage)
Folding screen
Gilt chairs

Off stage: Large chicken drumstick (**Dame**)
Black bag with "swag" written on it (**Grab**)

Personal: **Lotaloot:** foot bandage and stick
Mr X: pistol
Nick: magnifying glass

Scene 2

Personal: **Mr X:** pistol

Scene 3

On stage: Low wall surmounted with ornate urns
Alcove containing a stone seat (secret passage)

Off stage: Lit sparklers (**Dancers** or **Children**) (optional)

Personal: **Mr X:** gag

Scene 4

Personal: **Mr X:** pistol
Caroline: gag

Scene 5

On stage: Large ornate chair with secret compartment in seat. *In it:* velvet
drawstring bag with jewels, local newspaper

Personal: **Lotaloot:** foot bandage
Mr X: dagger, pistol
Smash: dagger
Grab: dagger

Scene 6

NIL

Scene 7

On stage: Low wall surmounted with ornate urns
Alcove containing a stone seat (secret passage)

Off stage: Jewel bag (**Mr X**)
Rapier (**Dick**)

Personal: **Lotaloot:** foot bandage
                Mr X: dagger, pistol
                Male Guest: rapier

<h2 style="text-align:center">S<small>CENE</small> 8</h2>

Off stage: Song sheet (**Chorus** or **Stage Management**)

<h2 style="text-align:center">S<small>CENE</small> 9</h2>

NIL

LIGHTING PLOT

Property fittings required: hanging chandelier
5 interior, 4 exterior settings

ACT I, Scene 1

To open: General exterior lighting

Cue 1	**Caroline** sings	(Page 15)
	Lighting becomes magical and dreamlike	
Cue 2	**Dick** retreats up stage	(Page 15)
	Return to previous lighting	
Cue 3	**Billy** faints	(Page 20)
	Quick black-out	

ACT I, Scene 2

To open: General exterior lighting

Cue 4	**Dick** exits	(Page 25)
	Fade to black-out	

ACT I, Scene 3

To open: General interior lighting

Cue 5	**The Singers** form a tableau	(Page 34)
	Fade to black-out	

ACT I, Scene 4

To open: Dark and mysterious lighting

Cue 6	**Mr X, Smash** and **Grab** exit *Lighting becomes brighter*	(Page 35)
Cue 7	**Lotaloot** exits *Lighting becomes dark and mysterious*	(Page 38)
Cue 8	**Mr X, Smash** and **Grab** exit *Fade to black-out*	(Page 38)

ACT I, SCENE 5

To open: General interior lighting

No cues

ACT II, SCENE 1

To open: General interior lighting, with moonlight effect outside

Cue 9	**Dame:** "What's that?!" *Lighting becomes dark and mysterious*	(Page 48)
Cue 10	Fireplace opens *Eerie, greenish light in the passage behind*	(Page 48)
Cue 11	**Mr X** closes the fireplace *Cut eerie lighting*	(Page 48)
Cue 12	**Mr X** opens the fireplace *Eerie, greenish light in the passage behind*	(Page 49)
Cue 13	The fireplace closes *Cut eerie lighting and return to normal*	(Page 49)
Cue 14	**Mr X** opens the fireplace *Eerie, greenish light in the passage behind*	(Page 52)
Cue 15	The fireplace closes *Cut eerie lighting and return to normal*	(Page 53)
Cue 16	At end of Song 11 *Fade to black-out*	(Page 55)

ACT II, Scene 2

To open: Dark and eerie interior lighting

Cue 17   **Dame** exits   (Page 61)
            Fade to black-out

ACT II, Scene 3

To open: Bright moonlit exterior with strong lighting from house windows

Cue 18   **Dick** and **Caroline** gaze at each other   (Page 63)
            Fireworks effect on backcloth

Cue 19   At start of Song 13   (Page 64)
            *Dim out stage lighting and make special use of
               fireworks effects on backcloth*

Cue 20   At end of Song 13   (Page 64)
            *Revert to previous lighting and continue spasmodic
               fireworks effect until end of scene*

Cue 21   The panel closes   (Page 67)
            *Bring up fireworks light effects to full, then fade to
               black-out*

ACT II, Scene 4

To open: Dark and eerie interior lighting

Cue 22   **Dame** hauls **Billy** out   (Page 72)
            Fade to black-out

ACT II, Scene 5

To open: Dim and spooky interior lighting

Cue 23   **The Thing** reads the newspaper   (Page 78)
            Fade to black-out

ACT II, SCENE 6

To open: Moonlit exterior

Cue 24   **Dick** runs out   (Page 81)
           Fade to black-out

ACT II, SCENE 7

To open: Bright moonlit exterior with lighting from house windows

No cues

ACT II, SCENE 8

To open: General lighting

Cue 25   **Daisy** trots off   (Page 89)
           Fade to black-out

ACT II, SCENE 9

To open: Full general lighting

No cues

EFFECTS PLOT

ACT I

Cue 1   **Caroline** sings   (Page 15)
            Ground mist

ACT II

Cue 2   **Dame**: "What's that?!"   (Page 48)
            Metallic, clicking noise behind the fireplace

Cue 3   **Dame**: "Go!"   (Page 50)
            Recorded high speed music (a 33 1/3 RPM record of
               Khachaturian's Sabre Dance *played at 45 RPM)*
            or live "hurry" music

Cue 4   **Dame** and **Billy** hold each other up   (Page 50)
            Cut recording or live music

Cue 5   **All**: "'Elp!" etc.   (Page 57)
            Footsteps stop. Loud grinding sound, off R

Cue 6   **All** dance with joy   (Page 57)
            Grinding sound stops with a thud

Cue 7   **Mr X** stamps his foot three times   (Page 57)
            Grinding sound and thud, off R

Cue 8   **Mr X** stamps his foot three times   (Page 58)
            Grinding sound and thud, off R

Cue 9   **Mr X** exits   (Page 58)
            Grinding sound and thud, off R

Cue 10   **All** stamp on the ground   (Page 60)
            Grinding sound, off R